risotto

D1299617

risotto

hamlyn

First published in 2002
by Hamlyn
a division of Octopus Publishing Group Ltd
2–4 Heron Quays, London E14 4JP

ISBN 0 600 60700 3

A CIP catalogue for this book is available from the British Library

Printed and bound in China

NOTES

1 The FDA advises that eggs should not be consumed raw. This book contains some dishes made with raw or lightly cooked eggs. It is prudent for more vulnerable people such as pregnant and nursing mothers, invalids, the elderly, babies and young children to avoid uncooked or lightly cooked dishes made with eggs.

2 Meat and poultry should be cooked thoroughly. Keep refrigerated until ready for cooking. To test if poultry is cooked, pierce the flesh through the thickest part with a skewer or fork—the juices should run clear, never pink or red.

3 This book includes dishes made with nuts and nut derivatives. It is advisable for those with known allergic reactions to nuts and nut derivatives and those who may be potentially vulnerable to these allergies, such as pregnant and nursing mothers, invalids, the elderly, babies, and children, to avoid dishes made with nuts and nut oils. It is also prudent to check the labels of preprepared ingredients for the possible inclusion of nut derivatives.

Contents

Introduction

Rice is to northern Italy what pasta is to the southern regions—it's the most widely used and popular staple food. It appears on lunch and dining tables as an accompaniment or as a course in its own right, unless soup is being served first. But every Italian is a born gourmet and no one would dream of serving food on a bed of plain, boiled rice, no matter how rich and elaborate the main dish.

Accordingly, Italian cooks invented risotto—literally meaning "little rice". Risottos, or more correctly *risotti*, may be simply flavored with herbs, spices, a little cheese, tomatoes or other vegetables, or they can be rich and elaborate combinations of meat, fish, shellfish, chicken, vegetables, cream, cheese, mushrooms, and dozens of other ingredients. What they all have in common is the unique creamy texture of the rice and a perfect balance of aromas and flavors.

What is risotto?

It is probably easier to define what risotto is not rather than what it is. It is not simply any old mixture of rice and other ingredients and it is never made from leftovers. It is fundamentally a savory rice dish, carefully flavored with other ingredients—sometimes only one or two, sometimes more—cooked in a very specific way so that the flavors combine and meld. It takes time, care, and an

intuitive ability to "feel" how the dish is developing as it cooks to make the perfect risotto. Both the technique (see page 14) and the type of rice (see page 10) are crucial to its success. Risotto's origins lie in the honorable tradition of peasant cookery, but this is far from saying it is an easy dish to perfect. On the contrary, an Italian cook will be judged by the quality of his or her risotto and it takes practice to match the standard.

Frugal cooks developed the idea of frying little risotto balls or cakes to use up leftover risotto and these have now become dishes in their own right. The popular appetizer *Arancini*, risotto balls filled with mozzarella cheese and then deep-fried, is actually a Sicilian recipe, but it has been enthusiastically adopted by the north, where it is known as *Supplì al Telefono*, telephone wires.

Italians also use rice for desserts and sweet dishes. While rice tarts and cakes are more popular, risotto-style rice puddings are also frequently made.

Risotto—history and tradition

It is impossible to say when or by whom risotto was created, and the great cities of the north—among them Milan, Venice, Bologna, and Verona, as well as Rome— all claim to be its birthplace. The dish was certainly known in Milan in the sixteenth century. Italy's cuisine is one of the most

venerable in Europe, tracing its origins back through ancient Rome to classical Greece and beyond. Alexander the Great invaded India in 326 B.C. and his army is known to have brought rice back with them to Europe. Much later, in the eleventh century, the Crusaders and their enemies, the Saracens, also imported rice from the Middle East. The round grain rice used for risotto first appeared in Italy in the fifteenth century and its cultivation was fostered by the powerful Sforza Dukes of Milan. Certainly, rice is a long-established European staple and has been successfullly cultivated in the Po valley since the sixteenth century. Italian rice became so famous that its export was banned by law. Even so, Thomas Jefferson, founding father of the American constitution and the republic's third president, smuggled two sacks of Italian rice out of the Piedmont back to his home in Virginia to cultivate on his estate. Italy remains today the largest producer of rice in Europe.

To understand how this humble, rather bland grain became transformed into one of the world's most famous and popular dishes means learning how Italians feel about cooking and food in general. Eating, especially with all the family gathered together, is regarded as one of life's great pleasures. Even in today's busy world, a relaxed two- or three-hour weekend lunch with several generations of aunts and

uncles, cousins, nephews and nieces, grandparents, and babies is still the social high point of many Italian calendars, although it may no longer be a weekly event. While catching up with each other's news and laughing and joking are an integral part of it, the meal itself lies at the heart of the occasion and the quality must be impeccable. Time spent at the market and in the kitchen is regarded as well spent and each dish is savored and appreciated by all the diners. For Italians, choosing ingredients and cooking them are acts of love and never a chore.

Almost more than any other cuisine in the world, Italian cooking is based around the seasons. Fruit and vegetables in particular are used at their youngest and freshest, but care is also taken that fish, cheese, meat, poultry, and herbs are in peak condition before they are even offered for sale. Although modern transportation means that most produce can be available almost anywhere in the world at any time of year, there is still a strong tradition, especially outside large cities, of using foods in season. This, in turn, generates an understanding of which ingredients have a natural affinity with each other and which combinations work best. Seafood, for example, is never served with cheese, as the flavors are not considered complementary and the mixture is indigestible. The tendency of foreigners to sprinkle quantities of grated Parmesan over every risotto served to

them, including mussel, squid, and clam, evokes expressions of horror and outrage on the faces of any Italian observers.

Risotto was born out of this combination of a joyous delight in preparing and cooking food and a seasonal approach to ingredients. To serve plain rice would indicate a lack of care and interest in the food and, by implication, in the people who were to eat it. Perhaps the first risotto simply consisted of rice, cooked in stock to add flavor, with butter and cheese stirred in, for the northern regions are also dairy farming country. From here, it was a small step to the inclusion of sun-ripened tomatoes, lightly sautéed fennel, freshly caught mussels, or succulent Parma ham.

Italian cooking, even today, is distinctly regional and, in some cases, even local. For centuries cooks have perfected their local specialties, passing the recipes down through the generations. Classic risottos all feature ingredients characteristic of northern Italy—butter, rather than olive oil, freshwater and sea fish, highly seasoned sausages and salami, Gorgonzola and Parmesan cheese, game, asparagus, herbs, mushrooms, and truffles. Rivalry between the regions is intense, with both Lombardy and the Veneto claiming "ownership" of more than fifty classic risotto recipes. The Veneto is famous for its seafood risottos and is also home to

Risi e Bisi, a risotto made with fresh green peas that was always served at the Doge's annual St. Mark's banquet in Venice. Golden-colored, saffron-flavored Risotto alla Milanese or Risotto Giallo is probably the best-known risotto in the world and Lombardy also boasts a superb and unusual lemon risotto. The Piedmont transforms a simple Risotto Bianco (see page 14)—rice, shallots, Parmesan cheese, and butter—into a gourmet dish by grating fragrant, locally grown white truffles on top.

It was at the comparatively late date of 1861 that Italy became a unified state, but cooking, as with many other important aspects of Italian daily life, remained firmly based in the regions. An invisible culinary frontier continued to separate the north from the south, which was eventually breached by the Tuscans. Gradually an interchange of ingredients, techniques, and dishes took place and today rice is served throughout the south and pasta has found its way to the north. Risotto is now known throughout the world and a new generation of chefs has created exotic recipes that are a far cry from the simple peasant dish, based on fresh local produce, that it once was. Yet even these risottos with lobster, mangoes, soy sauce, or vodka are true to the traditional technique and prepared with the same devoted attention.

Essential Ingredients

Risotto rice

Italian rice is a medium grain that is larger than round-grain or pudding rice and rounder than long-grain rice. There are four sub-categories of Italian rice: semifino is best used in soups, ordinario is ideal for puddings, rice tarts, and cakes, while fino and superfino are used for risottos. Generally speaking, the better the quality of the rice, the longer the cooking time. Superfino requires about 20 minutes, while ordinario needs only about 12 minutes. Probably the best-known superfino rice is arborio, which is extensively farmed and widely exported. Other superfino varieties include Carnaroli, Roma and Maratelli. A useful fino, which has slightly longer grains than superfino, is Vialone Nano. Sometimes packets are just labeled "risotto rice", but it is worth keeping an eye out for these specific varieties.

The secret of risotto rice lies in the capacity of the grains to absorb very large quantities of liquid, whether wine, stock, or water, swelling to about three times their original size without becoming soggy. The rice cooks to a wonderful creamy texture, but at the same time retains firmness and "bite". Like pasta, it is cooked until it is "al dente"—to the tooth. Unlike some other types of rice, risotto rice should never be rinsed before cooking, as this washes away the starch —a self-defeating act because the high starch content is what creates the special texture. Easy-cook risotto rice is also available, but it does not produce the authentic creaminess characteristic of the dish and is hardly any more convenient to use than standard risotto rice.

Store rice in a sealed container in a cool, dry place. It will keep for several months.

The first rule for making a perfect risotto is to use a fino or superfino rice. You can produce a passable risotto-style dish with long-grain rice, but it will not have the same texture and is liable to stick to the bottom of the saucepan.

Tomatoes

Like any dish, risotto is only as good as the quality of the original ingredients. Whatever these are, they should be as fresh as possible. This is particularly true of vegetables. If you are using fresh tomatoes, try to obtain sun-ripened ones, which have a sweeter, fuller flavor than those grown under glass. Vine tomatoes are usually sun-ripened, but more expensive. Plum tomatoes, a classic Italian ingredient, are less watery than many other varieties.

Herbs

Fresh herbs are always preferable to dried. If you cannot obtain fresh ones, look for freeze-dried herbs, which often have a better flavor, color, and texture than conventionally dried ones. If you are substituting dried herbs for fresh, use only a third of the quantity. Italian parsley is the flat leaf variety. Do not chop basil, as the delicate leaves are easily bruised. Tear it into small pieces instead.

Spices

As a rule, few spices are featured in risottos, but two—chilies and saffron—do play important roles. Dried red chilies, known as *peperoncini*, are a speciality of the Abruzzi. They are extremely fiery and nicknamed *diavoletti*, little devils. Saffron plays the starring role in the classic *Risotto alla Milanese* (see page 92) and is widely used in seafood risottos. It has a special affinity with mussels. It is the world's most expensive spice—at one time stealing it was a capital offense in Italy—but there is no substitute. Be wary about buying cheaper saffron, which may turn out to be safflower. It is similar in appearance, but paler than the orange-red saffron and, although it adds color to risotto, it will not add flavor. Fortunately, only a small quantity of saffron is required. Crush the threads and infuse them in water or stock before adding to the dish. Saffron powder is also available, but this may be adulterated with safflower.

Cheese

Many risottos call for grated Parmesan cheese. It is best to buy this in a block and grate it freshly when it is required, rather than using ready-grated Parmesan, which quickly becomes tasteless. Look for Parmesan with Parmigiano Reggiano stamped on the rind, which means that it comes from a strictly defined area between Parma and Modena and is a guarantee of quality. If you buy it from a delicatessen or specialist cheese shop, a wedge will be freshly cut from the cheese wheel and this will have a better flavor and texture than pre-packed cheese. It can be stored, wrapped in foil or cheesecloth, in the refrigerator for at least a month. Other Italian cheeses you may need include mozzarella, fontina, mascarpone and Gorgonzola. The best mozzarella, di bufala, is made from water buffalo milk. Fontina is creamy cheese produced in the Val d'Aosta in the Italian Alps. Mascarpone is very rich, triple-cream cheese from Lombardy and Gorgonzola is one of the world's great veined cheeses. It was once produced in the village of Gorgonzola—the cheese's full name is Stracchino Gorgonzola—now subsumed by suburban Milan and is today made throughout Lombardy. Butter is essential for making risotto. Italians always cook with unsalted butter and this is generally best for risottos. However, you can use salted butter for most of the recipes in this book if you prefer, except where unsalted is particularly specified because salted butter would spoil the flavor of the dish.

Olive oil

There is no substitute for olive oil, which has a distinctive flavor. In fact, olive oils from different regions of Italy, let alone from other countries, have individual flavors. The most widely acclaimed Italian olive oils are from Liguria and Apulia. Extra virgin is the best quality and most expensive. It is made from the first cold pressing of olives and has a maximum acidity of 1 percent. Virgin olive oil, which may be subdivided into superfine, fine, and virgin, is also cold pressed and low in acidity. Anything simply labeled "pure olive oil" is refined oil that has probably been heat treated. It lacks character and flavor and is not worth buying. Light olive oil, produced from the last cold pressing, has a very mild flavor. Estate oils are the equivalent of château wines. They are made from olives grown on a single estate, usually hand-picked and pressed almost immediately. They are very fine, extremely expensive, and best reserved for salad dressings. The color of olive oil is no indication of its flavor or quality.

Lemons

It is best to buy unwaxed lemons if you need to grate the zest. Lemons are often treated with an ethylene gas to preserve their color and keep the skins looking fresh. When squeezing fruit for juice, first roll it over the work surface several times to increase the yield.

Mushrooms

Italians are enthusiastic gatherers of mushrooms, so wild mushrooms feature in many risotto recipes. If you are going to pick your own, you must be absolutely certain that you can identify them accurately (in Italy, the local pharmacy will most helpfully do this for you). Some poisonous fungi look very similar to edible varieties. Most supermarkets now stock a range of wild mushrooms, although this is something of a misnomer as many of these species are now cultivated. Nevertheless, they do have more flavor than the common cultivated mushroom. Never wash mushrooms, as they absorb water like a sponge and become soggy. Simply brush them gently or wipe with damp paper towels. Porcini mushrooms, also known as ceps, are a special favorite. They are available dried from both supermarkets and Italian delicatessens. Although they are expensive, you only need to use a very small quantity, as they have a strong flavor, accentuated by drying. To reconstitute dried porcini, place them in a small bowl and pour in enough hot water to cover. Set aside for about 20 minutes, until soft. Drain and use like fresh mushrooms. Reserve the soaking water, which has a concentrated mushroom flavor, and use as stock.

Most of the ingredients used in the recipes in this book are widely available from supermarkets. An Italian delicatessen would be a good place to buy any speciality ingredients, such as pancetta, Italian cheeses, and olive paste. You can also make olive paste yourself very easily by processing 1 pound of pitted black olives in a food processor while adding ½–¾ cup extra virgin olive oil through the feeder tube.

The importance of stock

Good quality light stock is essential for making risotto. Chicken and vegetable stock are most commonly used. Fish or shellfish stock give seafood risottos a wonderful flavor, but vegetable stock can be substituted. A light beef stock is used more rarely, but pork, lamb, and bacon stock are all too strong. (See pages 16–19 for stock recipes.)

Homemade stock is flavorsome, you know exactly what has gone into it and you can skim off the fat, so it is healthy too. It is not difficult to make, although some types do require long cooking. Make a big batch of stock to save time and freeze it in portions for future use.

If homemade stock is not available, you can use stock cubes or bouillon powder. It is worth spending the extra money on good quality brands and checking the labels before buying. Some stock cubes contain monosodium glutamate (MSG) and many are very high in salt.

When cooking risottos, always heat the stock in a separate pan to simmering point before adding it to the rice. Keep the stock at a gentle simmer throughout the process.

Equipment

You will need a large saucepan, with a lid, that can contain the rice once it has finished cooking, bearing in mind that the grains will swell to about three times their original size. It should be heavy-based—cast iron, copper, or heavy-gauge steel or aluminum—to prevent the risotto from sticking and burning. A nonstick pan is of no particular advantage. A pan with a curved or rounded base is ideal as it prevents the rice from sticking around the edge of the base. Some risottos in this book are cooked in a frying pan. Again, this should be large and heavy-based.

The stock is added to rice a ladleful at a time, so a soup ladle is essential. Most hold about ½ cup. A wooden or plastic handle is safer than a metal one, as you are more than likely to leave the ladle resting in the pan of hot stock while you are cooking.

Any other equipment required for cooking risotto is likely to be found in most kitchens already—a measuring cup and spoons, chopping board, and knives, a grater, and a wooden spoon. A food processor is useful, but not essential.

How to make the perfect risotto

All risottos are made in basically the same way. Risotto should be prepared immediately before serving, although there is a trick for partially cooking in advance (see below). The following recipe is a basic risotto with Parmesan, which illustrates the general technique for all risottos.

Risotto bianco

4½–5 cups Vegetable Stock
  (see page 19)
¼ cup butter, preferably unsalted
2 shallots, finely chopped
1½ cups risotto rice
⅔ cup dry white wine
⅓ cup Parmesan cheese,
  freshly grated
salt

1. Bring the stock to simmering point in a large pan. The recipes in this book always specify precisely the quantity of stock. However, different varieties of risotto rice may absorb slightly more or less stock, so it is sensible to bring a little more than the specified amount to simmering point. Then, if you do need more stock, it is already hot. Note that, in the recipes, the stock is almost invariably listed in the ingredients as "hot stock" and this step does not then appear in the method.

Step-by-Step Risotto

2. Melt half the butter in a large, heavy-based pan over a low heat. (Some recipes specify butter, some olive oil, and others a mixture of the two.) Add the shallots (most savory risottos include at least one member of the onion family) and sauté gently. Cook them over a low heat, stirring occasionally, for about 5 minutes, until softened and translucent, but not colored. It is important that the onion is properly softened at this stage because although it will continue to cook, it will not soften further once the rice has been added. A tip is to add a pinch of salt when you start to sauté the onion, this will release the moisture and will keep it from cooking too quickly.

3. Add the rice to the pan and stir constantly with a wooden spoon over a low heat for 1–2 minutes, until all the grains are coated with butter and have become translucent. At this point they will be beginning to stick to the base of the pan.

4. Pour in the wine and bring to a boil over a medium heat, stirring constantly. Cook, stirring constantly, until almost all the liquid has evaporated. (Not every recipe includes wine and in some recipes it is simply heated with the stock.)

5. Add a ladleful of the simmering stock and cook over a medium heat, stirring constantly, until it has been completely absorbed by the rice. Continue adding the stock, 1 ladleful at a time, and continue cooking and stirring. Make sure that each addition of stock has been completely absorbed before you add any more. The liquid should be at a fairly vigorous simmer, so adjust the heat if necessary. Until you feel confident about making risottos, it is sensible to stir constantly throughout the cooking process. However, once you are more familiar with the "feel" of the rice, you can stir constantly to begin with and then only frequently after about 10 minutes. The purpose of stirring is to release the starch, as well as to prevent the rice from sticking to the base of pan, although Italian cooks will tell you that a perfect risotto just catches on the base. You may need to add a little more stock than specified in the recipes if the mixture becomes dry (see step 1). It will take about 20 minutes for the rice to cook. The grains should be plump and tender, but still firm, and the texture should be creamy.

6. Remove the pan from the heat and stir in the remaining butter and the Parmesan. This is called the *mantecatura*.

Cover the pan and leave the risotto to rest for 2–3 minutes. During this time, the butter and Parmesan will melt. Remove the lid and stir vigorously to increase the creaminess and serve immediately.

Part cooking risotto in advance

Ideally, risotto should always be made just before it is to be served, but as it requires constant attention, it can be frustrating when you are entertaining unless your guests are happy to keep you company in the kitchen. The technique described below is quite a successful way of cheating.

Prepare the risotto up to the point where you have sautéed the rice and the grains are well coated in butter or oil. Add 2 ladlefuls of hot stock and, when it has returned to the boil, cover the pan tightly and turn off the heat. If necessary for a firm seal, wrap a dish towel around the saucepan lid first. When you are ready to resume cooking, the rice will have absorbed all the stock and will be half cooked. Stir in a pat of butter and continue adding stock, 1 ladleful at a time, stirring constantly over a medium heat. The rice will take about 10 minutes more to cook.

Stocks

**Makes about 6 cups/ Preparation time: 10 minutes, plus cooling/
Cooking time: 35 minutes**

Fish Stock

1. Put the fish heads, bones, and trimmings in a large stock pot and add the onion, carrot, celery, herbs, and peppercorns. Pour in the wine and water.
2. Bring to a boil, cover, and simmer over a low heat for 30 minutes.
3. Remove the pot from the heat and strain. Cover, leave to cool, then store in the refrigerator until needed or freeze.

2 pounds heads, bones, and trimmings of white fish,
   rinsed in cold water
1 onion, finely chopped
1 carrot, thinly sliced
1 celery stick, thinly sliced
6 parsley sprigs
1 thyme sprig
1 fennel sprig
6 black peppercorns
⅔ cup dry white wine
7½ cups water

**Makes about 2½ quarts/ Preparation time: 15 minutes, plus chilling/
Cooking time: 3½ hours**

Chicken Stock

3 pounds chicken wings and necks

2 onions, cut into wedges

4½ quarts water

2 carrots, chopped

2 celery sticks, chopped

10 parsley sprigs

2 thyme sprigs

2 bay leaves

10 black peppercorns

1. Put the chicken wings and necks and the onions in a large, heavy-based stock pot. Cook over a low heat, stirring frequently, until lightly browned all over.
2. Add the water and bring to a boil, scraping up any sediment from the base of the pot with a wooden spoon. Skim off the scum that rises to the surface. Add the carrots, celery, parsley, thyme, bay leaves, and peppercorns, cover partially and simmer gently for 3 hours.
3. Remove the pot from the heat and strain the stock. Cover, leave to cool, then chill in the refrigerator overnight. Remove and discard the layer of fat that will have set on the surface.

Stocks

Makes about 2 quarts/ Preparation time: 20 minutes, plus chilling/ Cooking time: 5¼ hours

Beef Stock

3½ pounds beef bones, chopped into
   3-inch pieces

2 onions, quartered

2 carrots, chopped

2 celery sticks, chopped

2 tomatoes, chopped

4½ quarts water

10 parsley sprigs

4 thyme sprigs

2 bay leaves

8 black peppercorns

1. Put the beef bones into a large roasting pan and roast in a preheated oven at 450°F for 30 minutes, until lightly browned. Turn the bones occasionally during cooking. Add the onions, carrots, celery and tomatoes, spoon over the fat in the pan and roast, stirring occasionally, for a further 30 minutes.

2. Using a slotted spoon, transfer the bones and vegetables to a large stock pot. Drain off the fat from the roasting pan and add ⅔ cup of the water. Set the roasting pan over a low heat and bring to a boil, scraping up any sediment from the base of the pan. Pour this into the pot and add the remaining water.

3. Bring to a boil, skimming off the scum that rises to the surface. Add the parsley, thyme, bay leaves, and peppercorns. Partially cover the pan, lower the heat and simmer for 4 hours.

4. Strain the stock, cover, and leave to cool. Chill in the refrigerator overnight, then remove and discard the layer of fat that will have set on the surface.

**Makes about 2½ cups/ Preparation time: 5 minutes, plus cooling/
Cooking time: 30 minutes**

Vegetable Stock

¼ cup butter

2 onions, chopped

2 leeks, thinly sliced

2 carrots, chopped

2 celery sticks, chopped

1 fennel bulb, chopped

1 thyme sprig

1 marjoram sprig

1 fennel sprig

4 parsley sprigs

3¾ cups water

1. Melt the butter in a large, heavy-based saucepan. Add the onions, leeks, carrots, celery, and fennel, stir well to coat, then cover and cook over a low heat for 10 minutes.
2. Stir in the herbs and add the water. Bring to a boil, cover, and simmer for 15 minutes.
3. Remove the pan from the heat and strain the stock. Cover, leave to cool, then store in the refrigerator until needed or freeze.

Vegetables

Green Vegetable Risotto

A quick and easy risotto, this is the perfect choice if you are making a risotto for the first time.

½ cup butter

2 tablespoons olive oil

1 garlic clove, crushed and chopped

1 onion, finely diced

1½ cups risotto rice

4½ cups hot Chicken or Vegetable Stock (see
  pages 17 and 19)

4 ounces French beans, trimmed and cut into
  1-inch pieces

1 cup shelled peas

1 cup shelled and skinned fava beans

4 ounces asparagus, trimmed and cut into
  1-inch pieces

4 ounces baby spinach, washed and chopped

⅓ cup dry vermouth or white wine

¼ cup chopped parsley

½ cup Parmesan cheese, freshly grated

salt and pepper

1. Melt ¼ cup of the butter with the olive oil in a heavy-based saucepan. Add the garlic and onion and sauté gently for 5 minutes, but do not allow to brown.
2. Add the rice and stir well to coat the grains with the butter and oil. Add the hot stock, a large ladleful at a time, stirring until each addition is absorbed into the rice. Continue adding stock in this way, cooking until the rice is creamy but the grains are still firm. This should take about 20 minutes.
3. When you add the last of the stock, add the vegetables and vermouth or white wine, mix well, and cook for 2 minutes.
4. Remove the pan from the heat, season with salt and pepper and add the remaining butter, the chopped parsley, and Parmesan. Mix well, then cover and leave the risotto to rest for a few minutes before serving.

Spring Greens and Goat Cheese Risotto

½ cup extra virgin olive oil

2 leeks, sliced

2 garlic cloves, chopped

1¼ cups risotto rice

⅔ cup dry white wine

5 cups hot Vegetable Stock
  (see page 19)

8 ounces broccoli, cut into florets

8 ounces baby spinach, shredded

2 tablespoons chopped mixed herbs (such as
  basil, chives, mint, parsley, and tarragon)

4 ounces soft goat cheese, mashed

¼ cup Parmesan cheese, freshly grated

salt and pepper

1. Heat the oil in a large saucepan and sauté the leeks and garlic for 5 minutes, until softened. Add the rice and stir well to coat the grains with the oil. Add the wine, bring to a boil, and cook, stirring, until almost all the liquid has evaporated.

2. Add the hot stock, a ladleful at a time, stirring until each addition has been absorbed into the rice. Continue adding the stock in this way, cooking until the rice is creamy but the grains are still firm. This should take about 20 minutes. Add the broccoli to the rice after 12 minutes.

3. Stir the spinach, herbs, and both cheeses into the rice. Season to taste with salt and pepper and cook for a final 2 minutes until the spinach is wilted. Cover the pan and leave the risotto to rest for a few minutes before serving.

Fava Bean, Lemon, and Parmesan Risotto

This is a wonderfully fragrant dish that is lovely when fava beans are first in season.

1 tablespoon butter

¼ cup olive oil

1 onion, chopped

2 garlic cloves, crushed

2 cups risotto rice

⅔ cup dry white wine

5 cups hot Vegetable Stock (see page 19)

5 ounces fresh or frozen fava beans

¼ cup Parmesan cheese, freshly grated, plus
    extra to serve

finely grated zest and juice of 1 lemon

salt and pepper

thyme sprigs, to garnish

1. Melt the butter with the oil in a large, heavy-based saucepan. Add the onion and garlic and sauté gently for 5 minutes until softened but not colored. Add the rice and stir well to coat the grains with the butter and oil.

2. Add the wine, bring to a boil, and cook, stirring, until almost all the liquid has evaporated. Add the hot stock, a ladleful at a time, stirring until each addition is absorbed into the rice. Continue adding stock in this way, until half the stock has been used. Stir in the beans.

3. Gradually add the remaining stock, a ladleful at a time as before, cooking until the rice is creamy but the grains are still firm. This will take about 20 minutes in total. Stir in the Parmesan, lemon zest and juice, and season to taste with salt and pepper. Cover the pan and leave the risotto to rest for a few minutes before serving with extra Parmesan and thyme sprigs.

Serves 4/ Preparation time: 5–10 minutes/ Cooking time: 30 minutes

Country-style Risotto

Known as *risotto alla rustica*, this simple dish is packed with flavor.

¼ cup olive oil

3 tablespoons butter

2 shallots, finely chopped

1 small onion, finely chopped

1 rosemary sprig, finely chopped

2 tablespoons finely chopped parsley

¼ teaspoon finely chopped marjoram

4 basil leaves, finely chopped

1 garlic clove, crushed

1¾ cups risotto rice

¼ cup dry white wine

4 plum tomatoes, skinned

3½ cups hot Vegetable Stock (see page 19)

¼ cup light cream

salt and pepper

1. Heat the oil and all but 1 teaspoon of the butter in a large heavy-based saucepan over a low heat. Add the shallots, onions, herbs, and garlic and cook over a medium heat, stirring occasionally, for 5 minutes.
2. Add the rice, stir well to coat the grains with the butter and oil. Pour in the wine, bring to a boil, and cook, stirring, until almost all the liquid has evaporated. Add the tomatoes, mashing with a fork. Mix thoroughly.
3. Add the hot stock, a large ladleful at a time, stirring until each addition is absorbed into the rice. Continue adding stock in this way, cooking until the rice is creamy but the grains are still firm. This should take about 20 minutes.
4. As the rice becomes creamy, add the reserved butter and plenty of pepper. Stir in the cream just before serving.

Lemon, Leek, and Bay Leaf Risotto

The addition of bay to this lemon risotto imparts a wonderful flavor and aroma. This dish is a good accompaniment to grilled fish or shellfish.

¼ cup butter

1 onion, finely chopped

2 garlic cloves, crushed

2 leeks, trimmed, washed, and sliced

1¼ cups risotto rice

6 bay leaves, bruised

⅔ cup dry vermouth

4½–5 cups hot Chicken Stock or Vegetable Stock
(see pages 17 and 19)

juice and zest of 1 large lemon

¼ cup mascarpone cheese

¼ cup Parmesan cheese, freshly grated, plus
extra for serving

salt and pepper

1. Melt the butter in a heavy-based saucepan. Add the onion, garlic, and leeks and sauté for 10 minutes, until softened but not browned. Add the rice and bay leaves and stir well to coat the grains with the butter. Add the vermouth, bring to a boil, and cook until the liquid has reduced by half.

2. Add the hot stock, a ladleful at a time, stirring until each addition is absorbed into the rice. Continue adding stock in this way, cooking until the rice is creamy but the grains are still firm. This should take about 20 minutes.

3. Add the lemon juice and zest, season to taste with salt and pepper, and stir for a further 5 minutes. Add the mascarpone and Parmesan, stir once, cover, and leave the risotto to rest for a few minutes before serving with grated Parmesan.

Lemon and Thyme Risotto with Vodka

A wonderfully light and fragrant risotto. Serve on its own or as an accompaniment to a meat or fish dish.

½ cup butter

6 scallions or young shallots, finely chopped

⅔ cup dry white wine

finely grated zest and juice of 1 large lemon

2½ cups risotto rice

6¼ cups hot Chicken or Vegetable Stock (see
pages 17 and 19)

¼ cup vodka

2 tablespoons chopped thyme

⅓ cup Parmesan cheese, freshly grated

salt and pepper

TO GARNISH:

thyme sprigs

strips of lemon zest

1. Melt half of the butter in a large heavy-based saucepan, add the scallions or shallots and sauté for 5 minutes, until soft. Pour in the wine, add half the lemon zest, bring to a boil, and cook, stirring, until almost all the liquid has evaporated.

2. Add the rice and stir well to coat the grains with the butter. Add the hot stock, a large ladleful at a time, stirring until each addition is absorbed into the rice. Continue adding stock in this way, cooking until the rice is creamy, but the grains are still firm. This should take about 20 minutes. Season to taste with salt and pepper. Stir in the remaining butter and lemon rind, the lemon juice, vodka, thyme, and Parmesan.

3. Cover the pan and leave the risotto to rest for a few minutes before serving, garnished with thyme sprigs and strips of lemon zest.

Serves 4/ Preparation time: 10 minutes/ Cooking time: 45–50 minutes

Roasted Garlic and Leek Risotto

The garlic-infused oil adds an intense aroma and flavor to the risotto, while the deep-fried leeks give it an attractive appearance, making this an ideal dish to serve to guests.

6 large garlic cloves

about ⅔ cup olive oil

1 pound medium leeks, plus 2 extra to garnish

vegetable oil, for deep-frying

2½ cups risotto rice

6¼ cups hot Chicken or Vegetable Stock (see pages 17 and 19)

¼ cup Parmesan cheese, freshly grated

salt and pepper

1. Put the garlic cloves into a small saucepan. Cover completely with the olive oil and bring to a simmer. Simmer gently for about 20 minutes, or until the garlic is golden and soft. Leave the garlic to cool in the oil. Remove the garlic cloves once cool and set aside.

2. Meanwhile cut the 2 leeks for the garnish into 3-inch lengths, then slice them in half lengthwise and cut into long thin shreds. Deep-fry the shredded leeks for 1–2 minutes until crisp and just golden. Lift them out of the oil with a slotted spoon and drain on paper towels. Slice the remaining leeks.

3. Heat ⅓ cup of the garlic-flavored olive oil in a heavy-based saucepan. Add the sliced leeks and sauté for a few minutes until they are beginning to soften and color slightly, then stir in the reserved garlic cloves.

4. Add the rice and stir well to coat the grains with the oil. Add the stock, a large ladleful at a time, stirring until each addition is absorbed into the rice. Continue adding stock in this way, cooking until the rice is creamy, but the grains are still firm. This should take about 20 minutes. Season well, stir in the Parmesan, and cover the pan. Leave the risotto to rest for a few minutes before serving, garnished with a tangle of fried leeks.

Pumpkin, Sage, and Chili Risotto

½ cup butter

1 large onion, finely chopped

1–2 fresh or dried red chilies, seeded and finely chopped

1 pound pumpkin, peeled and roughly chopped

2½ cups risotto rice

6¼ cups hot Chicken or Vegetable Stock (see pages 17 and 19)

⅓ cup chopped sage

⅓ cup Parmesan cheese, freshly grated

salt and pepper

sage sprigs, to garnish

1. Heat half the butter in a large saucepan and add the onion. Sauté over a low heat for 5 minutes until softened but not colored. Stir in the chilies and cook for 1 minute. Add the pumpkin and cook, stirring constantly, for 5 minutes.

2. Add the rice and stir well to coat the grains with the butter. Add the hot stock, a large ladleful at a time, stirring until each addition is absorbed into the rice. Continue adding stock in this way, cooking until the rice is creamy but the grains are still firm. This should take about 20 minutes and the pumpkin should start to disintegrate. Season to taste with salt and pepper, then stir in the sage, the remaining butter, and the Parmesan. Cover the pan and leave the risotto to rest for a few minutes before serving, garnished with sage sprigs.

Butternut Squash Risotto

1 butternut squash, weighing 2 pounds

⅓ cup olive oil

½ cup butter

1 garlic clove, finely chopped

1 onion, finely diced

1½ cups risotto rice

4½ cups hot Chicken or Vegetable stock (see
   pages 17 and 19)

⅔ cup Parmesan cheese, freshly grated

salt and pepper

pumpkin seed oil, to serve

1. Trim the squash, cut it through the middle, then pare away the skin from the larger half without losing too much of the flesh. Cut in half lengthwise, remove the seeds and cut the flesh into 2-inch dice. Repeat with the other piece. Place on a large baking sheet, drizzle with ¼ cup of the olive oil and season with salt and pepper. Mix well and cook in a preheated oven at 425°F for 15 minutes, until soft and slightly browned.

2. Melt ¼ cup of the butter with the remaining olive oil in a heavy-based saucepan. Add the garlic and onion and sauté gently for 5 minutes, until softened but not colored.

3. Add the rice and stir well to coat the grains with oil and butter. Add the hot stock a large ladleful at a time, stirring until each addition is absorbed into the rice. Continue adding stock in this way, cooking until the rice is creamy but the grains are still firm. This should take about 20 minutes.

4. Remove the squash from the oven, add to the risotto with the Parmesan and remaining butter, season to taste with salt and pepper and stir gently. Cover the pan and leave the risotto to rest for a few minutes before serving with a little pumpkin seed oil drizzled on top of each portion.

Beet and Horseradish Risotto

This risotto makes an impressive main course for 4 people, but will also serve 6–8 as a colorful appetizer. If you can find fresh horseradish, use it in place of the bottled variety. The flavor is far superior, but beware of its heat intensity, which can range from harmlessly mild to hot and fiery, depending on how fresh it is.

½ cup olive oil

1 large red onion, chopped

3 garlic cloves, crushed

2 cups risotto rice

5½ cups hot Vegetable Stock
   (see page 19)

14 ounces cooked beets, finely diced

½ cup roughly chopped dill

2–4 cups freshly grated horseradish or
   2 tablespoons hot horseradish from a jar

½ cup salted macadamia nuts or almonds

salt and pepper

mixed salad leaves, to serve

1. Heat the oil in a large, heavy-based saucepan. Add the onion and garlic and sauté gently for 5 minutes until softened but not colored. Add the rice and stir well to coat the grains with the oil.
2. Add the hot stock, a large ladleful at a time, stirring until each addition is absorbed into the rice. Continue adding stock in this way, cooking until the rice is creamy but the grains are still firm. This should take about 20 minutes.
3. Stir in the beet, dill, horseradish, and nuts. Season to taste with salt and pepper and heat through gently for 2–3 minutes. Cover the pan and leave the risotto to rest for a few minutes before serving with mixed salad leaves.

Creamy Radicchio and Pancetta Risotto

This unusual dish is from the Veneto, where rice is grown as well as several varieties of radicchio. It has both a sweet and a sharp flavor.

½ cup butter

2 carrots, finely diced

4 ounces smoked pancetta, finely diced

2 garlic cloves, finely chopped

1 pound radicchio, finely shredded

2½ cups risotto rice

6¼ cups hot Chicken or Vegetable Stock (see pages 17 and 19)

⅓ cup light cream

⅓ cup Parmesan cheese, freshly grated, plus extra to serve

salt and pepper

1. Melt half of the butter in a large saucepan and add the carrots. Cook gently for 5 minutes until they start to soften. Add the pancetta and garlic and cook until just beginning to color. Stir in the radicchio and cook until it begins to wilt.

2. Add the rice and stir well to coat the grains with the butter. Add the hot stock, a large ladleful at a time, stirring until each addition is absorbed into the rice. Continue adding stock in this way, cooking until the rice is creamy but the grains are still firm. This should take about 20 minutes. Season to taste with salt and pepper, then stir in the remaining butter, the cream, and Parmesan.

3. Cover the pan and leave the risotto to rest for a few minutes before serving, sprinkled with a little grated Parmesan.

Risotto with Red Pepper and Eggplant

This colorful risotto has a robust flavor and a deliciously rich texture.

¼ cup olive oil

3 tablespoons butter

1 shallot, finely chopped

1 eggplant, finely chopped

1 red bell pepper, cored, seeded, and finely
   diced

1¾ cups risotto rice

¼ cup dry white wine

4½ cups hot Vegetable Stock (see page 19)

2 tablespoons chopped parsley

4 basil leaves, torn into small pieces (see herbs,
   page 10)

2 tablespoons Parmesan cheese, freshly grated

¼ cup light cream

salt and pepper

1. Heat the oil and 2 tablespoons of the butter in a deep pan. Add the shallot and sauté over a medium heat for 3 minutes until softened, but not colored. Add the eggplant and diced pepper and cook over a medium high heat for about 5 minutes.

2. Add the rice and stir well to coat the grains with the butter and oil. Add the wine, bring to a boil, and cook, stirring, until almost all the liquid has evaporated. Add the hot stock, a large ladleful at a time, stirring until each addition is absorbed into the rice. Continue adding stock in this way, cooking until the rice is creamy but the grains are still firm. This should take about 20 minutes.

3. Season to taste with salt and pepper, if necessary. Add the reserved butter, chopped herbs, Parmesan, and cream. Mix well, cover, and leave the risotto to rest for a few minutes before serving.

Serves 6/ Preparation time: 20 minutes/ Cooking time: 30 minutes

Wild Mushroom Risotto

If you are not using ceps, try to obtain two or three different kinds of mushrooms to make a really flavorful dish. Alternatively, use a mixture of cultivated and wild mushrooms.

½ cup butter

1 large onion, finely chopped

2 garlic cloves, finely chopped

6 ounces mixed wild mushrooms or ceps, roughly chopped

2 tablespoons chopped mixed thyme and marjoram

⅔ cup dry white wine

2½ cups risotto rice

6¼ cups hot Chicken or Vegetable Stock (see pages 17 and 19)

salt and pepper

shredded marjoram leaves, to garnish

⅓ cup Parmesan cheese, freshly grated, to serve

1. Melt the butter in a large, heavy-based saucepan. Add the onion and garlic and sauté gently for 5 minutes, until softened, but not colored. Stir in the mushrooms and herbs, and cook over a moderate heat for 3 minutes. Pour in the wine, bring to a boil, and cook, stirring until almost all the liquid has evaporated.

2. Add the rice and stir well to coat the grains with the butter. Add the stock, a large ladleful at a time, stirring until each addition is absorbed into the rice. Continue adding the stock in this way, cooking until the rice is creamy but the grains are still firm. This should take about 20 minutes. Season to taste with salt and pepper.

3. Cover the pan and leave the risotto to rest for a few minutes, garnish with the shredded marjoram, then serve with the grated Parmesan.

Piedmontese Risotto

The Piedmont borders on both France and Switzerland and is a famous farming region of northern Italy. The word Piedmont literally means "foot of the mountains".

½ cup butter

1 large onion, finely chopped

⅔ cup dry white wine

2½ cups risotto rice

pinch of saffron threads

6¼ cups hot Chicken or Vegetable Stock (see
    pages 17 and 19)

⅓ cup Parmesan cheese, freshly grated

salt and pepper

1. Melt half of the butter in a large, heavy-based saucepan. Add the onion and sauté gently for 5 minutes, until softened but not colored. Pour in the wine, bring to a boil, and cook, stirring, until almost all the liquid has evaporated.

2. Add the rice and saffron and stir well to coat the grains with the butter. Add the stock, a large ladleful at a time, and stir until each addition is absorbed into the rice. Continue adding stock in this way, cooking until the rice is creamy but the grains are still firm. This should take about 20 minutes. Season to taste with salt and pepper, then stir in the remaining butter and the Parmesan.

3. Cover the pan and leave the risotto to rest for a few minutes, then serve.

Sage and Walnut Risotto with a Cheese Crust

Try to get the freshest walnuts possible for this classic combination, as walnuts that have been stored for a long time tend to be dry and bitter.

¼ cup butter

1 onion, chopped

1¾ cups risotto rice

5½ cups hot Vegetable Stock (see page 19)

¼ cup chopped sage

½ cup walnuts, roughly chopped

8 ounces Brie cheese, thinly sliced

salt and pepper

mixed salad leaves, to serve

1. Melt the butter in a large, heavy-based saucepan. Add the onion and sauté for 5 minutes, until softened but not browned. Add the rice and stir well to coat the grains with the butter.

2. Add the hot stock, a large ladleful at a time, stirring until each addition is absorbed into the rice. Continue adding stock in this way, cooking until the rice is creamy but the grains are still firm. This should take about 20 minutes.

3. Stir in the sage and walnuts and season to taste with salt and pepper. Transfer the risotto to a shallow flameproof serving dish and cover with the slices of Brie. Cook under a preheated hot broiler for about 3 minutes, until the cheese has melted. Serve with mixed salad leaves.

Onion Risotto with Sun-dried Tomatoes

2 tablespoons butter

¼ cup extra virgin olive oil

1 pound pearl onions

¼ cup chopped thyme

1¾ cups risotto rice

⅔ cup light red wine

3¾ cups Vegetable Stock (see page 19)

4 ounces drained sun-dried tomatoes in oil, chopped

2 tablespoons balsamic vinegar

½ cup crème fraîche

salt and pepper

grated Parmesan cheese, to serve

1. Melt the butter with the oil in a large frying pan, add the onions and cook over a low heat for 25 minutes until golden and caramelized, stirring occasionally.

2. Add the thyme and rice and stir well to coat the grains with the butter, oil, and onions, then pour in the red wine. Boil rapidly for 5 minutes until reduced. Add the hot stock, a large ladleful at a time, stirring until each addition is absorbed into the rice. Continue adding stock in this way, cooking until the rice is creamy but the grains are still firm. This should take about 20 minutes.

3. Stir in all the remaining ingredients, season to taste with salt and pepper and serve with Parmesan.

Herby Risotto

Toma cheese from the Italian Alps is used in this aromatic risotto. If you cannot find it, use fontina or Parmesan instead.

½ cup butter

¼ cup olive oil

1 onion, finely chopped

1 garlic clove, finely chopped

1½ cups risotto rice

4½ cups hot Chicken or Vegetable Stock (see pages 17 and 19)

handful of parsley, chopped

handful of basil, chopped

handful of oregano, chopped

handful of thyme, chopped

4 ounces Toma cheese, grated

salt and pepper

herb sprigs, to garnish

1. Melt ¼ cup of the butter with the olive oil in a heavy-based saucepan, add the onion and garlic and sauté for 5 minutes until softened but not colored.

2. Add the rice and stir well to coat the grains with the butter and oil. Add the hot stock, a large ladleful at a time, stirring until each addition is absorbed into the rice. Continue adding stock in this way, cooking until the rice is creamy but the grains are still firm. This should take about 20 minutes.

3. Add the herbs, the remaining butter, and the cheese and mix well. Season to taste with salt and pepper and stir well. Cover and leave the risotto to rest for a few minutes before serving, garnished with the herb sprigs.

Serves 4/ Preparation time: 10 minutes/ Cooking time: 25 minutes

Red Wine Risotto

2 cups Valpolicella or other red wine

2½ cups hot Chicken Stock (see page 17)

½ cup butter

2 tablespoons olive oil

2 garlic cloves, finely chopped

2 red onions, chopped

1½ cups risotto rice

8 ounces field mushrooms, trimmed and sliced

⅔ cup Parmesan cheese, freshly grated

salt and pepper

1. Heat the red wine in a large saucepan to a gentle simmer. Add the hot stock.

2. Melt ¼ cup of the butter with the oil in a heavy-based saucepan. Add the garlic and onions and sauté gently for 5 minutes, until softened but not colored.

3. Add the rice and stir well to coat the grains with the butter and oil. Add the hot stock mixture, a large ladleful at a time, stirring until each addition is absorbed into the rice. Continue adding the stock mixture in this way, cooking until the rice is creamy but the grains are still firm. This should take about 20 minutes. When half of the stock has been incorporated, add the mushrooms and season to taste with salt and pepper.

4. When all the stock has been added and the rice is just cooked, add most of the Parmesan and the remaining butter and mix well. Cover and leave the risotto to rest for a few minutes, garnish with a little grated Parmesan and serve.

Chestnut Risotto Cakes

These delicious little cakes are crisp on the outside yet moist and risotto-like in the middle. If you do not need the whole quantity, freeze the shaped but uncooked mixture for a later date.

½ ounce dried porcini mushrooms

2 tablespoons olive oil

¾ cup risotto rice

2½ cups hot Vegetable Stock (see page 19)

¼ cup butter

1 onion, chopped

3 garlic cloves, crushed

7 ounces cooked, peeled chestnuts, chopped

⅓ cup freshly grated Parmesan cheese

1 egg, lightly beaten

¼ cup polenta or cornmeal

vegetable oil, for shallow-frying

salt and pepper

lemon wedges, to garnish

mixed salad leaves, to serve

1. Place the dried mushrooms in a bowl and cover with boiling water. Leave to stand while preparing the rice.
2. Heat the olive oil in a heavy-based saucepan. Add the rice and stir well to coat the grains with oil. Add the hot stock and bring to a boil. Reduce the heat, cover partially and simmer, stirring frequently, for 12–15 minutes, until the rice is tender and the stock is absorbed. Transfer to a bowl.
3. Meanwhile, melt the butter in a saucepan. Add the onion and garlic and sauté gently for 5 minutes. Drain and chop the mushrooms, then add them to the rice with the onion mixture, chestnuts, Parmesan, and egg. Stir until well combined and season to taste with salt and pepper.
4. Divide the mixture into 12 portions. Pat each portion into a cake and roll in the polenta. Heat the oil for shallow-frying and fry the cakes for 2 minutes on each side, until golden. Garnish each serving with a lemon wedge and serve immediately with mixed salad leaves.

Fish and Shellfish

Smoked Salmon Risotto with Dill and Crème Fraîche

3½ ounces smoked salmon

1 cup snow peas

¼ cup butter

3 shallots, finely chopped

1¾ cups risotto rice

5 cups hot Fish Stock (see page 16)

⅔ cup crème fraîche

¼ cup chopped dill

salt and pepper

1. Cut the salmon into small pieces. Slice the snow peas lengthwise into thin slices.
2. Melt the butter in a large, heavy-based saucepan and gently sauté the shallots for 5 minutes until softened but not colored. Add the rice and stir well to coat the grains with the butter.
3. Add the hot stock, a large ladleful at a time, stirring until each addition is absorbed into the rice. Continue adding stock in this way, cooking until the rice is creamy but the grains are still firm. This should take about 20 minutes.
4. Add the smoked salmon, shredded snow peas, and half the crème fraîche and dill, stirring gently for about 1 minute, until the salmon has turned opaque. Season to taste with salt and pepper. Cover and leave the risotto to rest for a few minutes, then spoon over the remaining crème fraîche, if desired, and serve scattered with the remaining dill.

Fish Risotto

¼–⅓ cup unsalted butter

1 large onion, finely chopped

1 celery stick, sliced

1 thyme sprig

2 parsley sprigs

1 mace blade

1 small onion, left whole and studded with
   2 cloves

5–6 cups hot Fish Stock (see page 16)

1¾–2½ cups risotto rice

⅔ cup dry white wine

1 pound monkfish, haddock, halibut, or other
   firm white fish fillets, skinned and cubed

2 small red mullet, heads and tails removed, cut
   into 1-inch slices (optional)

3–4 saffron threads (optional)

1 garlic clove, finely chopped

10 ounces cooked shrimp in their shells

3 tablespoons Parmesan cheese, freshly grated,
   plus extra to serve

sea salt and freshly ground white pepper

finely chopped parsley, to garnish

1. Heat 2 tablespoons of the butter in a large, heavy-based pan. Add the onion and sauté for 5 minutes, until softened but not colored.

2. Meanwhile, tie the celery, thyme, parsley, mace blade, and studded onion in a piece of cheesecloth and add to the pan of fish stock. Bring just to boiling point, then keep at a gentle simmer.

3. Add the rice (use a larger amount if omitting the mullet) to the onions and stir well to coat the grains with the butter. Pour in the wine, bring to a boil, and cook, stirring, until almost all the liquid has evaporated.

4. Add the hot stock, a large ladleful at a time, stirring until each addition is absorbed into the rice. Continue adding stock in this way until you have added about 4½ cups.

5. Add the monkfish and red mullet slices, if using, then pour in a little more stock and cook for 4–5 minutes.

6. Put the saffron, if using, in a small bowl, and pour over 3–4 tablespoons of the stock. Stir quickly to start the color running, then set aside.

7. Melt 1 tablespoon of the butter in a small pan, add the garlic and shrimp and cook for 3–4 minutes, then stir into the risotto. Add the saffron liquid and another ladleful of stock, cooking until the rice is creamy but the grains are still firm. Season to taste with salt and pepper.

8. Add the remaining butter and the Parmesan, stirring until melted. Cover and leave the risotto to rest for a few minutes before sprinkling with parsley and serving with more Parmesan.

Seafood Risotto

In an authentic Italian risotto, such as Fish Risotto on page 56, the stock is added a ladleful at a time and fully absorbed before more is added. In this simpler version, the stock is added all at once and simmered gently until all the liquid has been absorbed.

¼ cup butter

1 onion, chopped

1 yellow bell pepper, cored, seeded, and chopped

1 red bell pepper, cored, seeded, and chopped

4 tomatoes, skinned, seeded, and chopped

12 ounces cod, skinned and cut into bite-sized pieces

8 prepared scallops

1¼ cups risotto rice

2 cups hot Fish Stock (see page 16)

salt and pepper

2 tablespoons finely chopped parsley, to garnish

¼ cup freshly grated Parmesan cheese, to serve

1. Melt half of the butter in a heavy-based saucepan. Add the onion, yellow and red peppers, and tomatoes and sauté gently for 2 minutes until softened but not colored.

2. Add the cod and scallops, and cook for a further 3 minutes. Transfer to a bowl and season with salt and pepper. Cover and set aside.

3. Melt the remaining butter in the pan, add the rice, and stir well to coat the grains with the butter. Stir in the stock and 1 teaspoon of salt. Bring to a boil, lower the heat, and cover the pan. Simmer for 15 minutes, until the rice is almost tender and the liquid has been absorbed.

4. Gently stir in the cod mixture and heat for 2 minutes. Garnish the risotto with parsley, sprinkle with Parmesan cheese, and serve immediately.

Serves 6/ Preparation time: 25 minutes/ Cooking time: 1 hour

Saffron Seafood Risotto

2 large pinches of saffron threads

12 ounces raw shrimp in their shells

6¼ cups hot Fish Stock (see page 16)

1¼ cups dry white wine

6 baby squid, cleaned

6 scallops

1 pound mussels

8 ounces small clams

⅓ cup butter

1 onion, finely chopped

2½ cups risotto rice

⅓ cup chopped parsley, to garnish

1. Put the saffron threads in a small bowl, cover with warm water, stir, and set aside to soak.
2. Remove the heads from the shrimp and put the heads into a large saucepan with the stock and wine. Bring to a boil, cover the pan, and simmer for 20 minutes.
3. Cut the squid into rings and trim the tentacles. Remove the hard white muscle from the side of each scallop. Scrub the mussels well and pull off any beards. Discard any with damaged shells or shells that do not close when sharply tapped. Rinse the clams well.
4. Strain the shrimp stock into a clean saucepan and bring to simmering point. Add the shrimp and cook for 2 minutes. Add the squid and scallops and cook for a further 2 minutes. Remove all the seafood with a slotted spoon and set aside. Put the mussels and clams into the stock and bring to a boil. Cover and cook for 5 minutes, or until all the shellfish have opened. Remove with a slotted spoon. Discard any that remain closed.
5. Melt the butter in a large saucepan. Add the onion and sauté for 5 minutes, until softened but not colored. Add the rice and stir well to coat the grains with the butter. Add the hot stock, a large ladleful at a time, stirring until each addition is absorbed into the rice. Continue adding stock in this way, cooking until only 2 ladlefuls of stock remain and the rice is creamy but the grains are still firm. This should take about 20 minutes. Season to taste with salt and pepper.
6. Finally, stir in the remaining stock, the infused saffron liquid, and all the seafood, cover and cook gently for 5 minutes, or until piping hot. Leave the risotto to rest for a few minutes before serving, sprinkled with the parsley.

Serves 4/ Preparation time: 10 minutes/ Cooking time: 30–35 minutes

Roast Cod and Olive Risotto

This dish would work equally well with most firm-fleshed white fish, such as monkfish or haddock.

1 pound cod fillet, skinned

2½ cups white wine

2½ cups hot Fish Stock (see page 16)

¼ cup butter

2 onions, chopped

1¾ cups risotto rice

2 ounces sun-dried tomatoes in oil, drained and
   sliced

½ cup olive oil

¼ cup chopped oregano

7 ounces cherry tomatoes, halved

¼ cup freshly grated Parmesan cheese

½ cup pitted black olives, chopped

2 tablespoons white wine vinegar

salt and pepper

1. Pat the fish dry on paper towels and cut into 4 pieces. Season with salt and pepper. Put the wine and stock in a saucepan and bring almost to a boil. Melt the butter in a large, heavy-based saucepan and sauté the onions for 5 minutes, until softened but not colored.

2. Add the rice and sun-dried tomatoes and stir well to coat the grains with the butter. Add the hot stock mixture, a large ladleful at a time, stirring until each addition is absorbed into the rice. Continue adding stock in this way, cooking until the rice is creamy but the grains are still firm. This should take about 20 minutes.

3. Meanwhile, heat ¼ cup of the oil in a large frying pan and cook the fish for 3 minutes on each side, until cooked through. Drain and keep warm. Add the oregano and cherry tomatoes to the pan and cook for 1 minute. Season lightly with salt and pepper.

4. Stir the cheese into the risotto and pile on to serving plates. Top with the fish and cherry tomatoes. Add the olives, the remaining oil, and the vinegar to the frying pan, stirring for a few seconds, then pour over the fish to serve.

Smoked Haddock Risotto

Smoked haddock is also known as finnan haddie.

1 pound smoked haddock fillet, skinned

5 cups water

2–3 saffron threads

2 tablespoons butter

4 shallots, finely chopped

2 garlic cloves, crushed

2 tablespoons chopped sage

1¾ cups risotto rice

⅔ cup dry white wine

½ cup crème fraîche or heavy cream

2 tablespoons freshly grated Parmesan cheese

¼ cup olive oil

12 large sage leaves

salt and pepper

1. Pull out and discard any bones that may remain in the haddock. Place the fish in a large frying pan and pour in the water. Bring to a boil over a low heat and simmer gently for 5 minutes. Lift out the fish, flake into large pieces, and set aside. Strain the cooking liquid into a saucepan and add the saffron threads. Leave to infuse for 10 minutes

2. Melt the butter in a large nonstick frying pan. Add the shallots, garlic, and sage and sauté for 5 minutes, until softened but not brown. Add the rice and stir well to coat the grains with the butter. Pour in the wine, bring to a boil, and cook, stirring, until almost all the liquid has evaporated.

3. Meanwhile, bring the saffron stock to a gentle simmer. Add the hot stock, a large ladleful at a time, stirring until each addition is absorbed into the rice. Continue adding stock in this way, cooking until the rice is creamy but the grains are still firm. This will take about 20 minutes.

4. Stir in the crème fraîche or heavy cream, Parmesan, and season to taste with salt and pepper and arrange the flaked fish on top. Cover loosely with foil. Heat the oil in a small frying pan and fry the sage leaves for 1 minute, until crispy. Serve the risotto garnished with the sage leaves.

Serves 4/ Preparation time: 10 minutes/ Cooking time: 20–25 minutes

Tuna and Fennel Risotto

Virtually a pantry staple, this risotto-style dish is a good choice for a midweek family supper.

2 tablespoons vegetable oil

1 onion, chopped

2 bacon slices, chopped

1 fennel bulb, chopped

4 ounces button mushrooms, sliced

1¼ cups long-grain rice

1 14-ounce can chopped tomatoes

2 teaspoons tomato paste

1¼ cups hot Vegetable Stock (see page 19)
   or water

grated zest of 1 lemon

2 tablespoons lemon juice

dash of Tabasco sauce

1 7-ounce can tuna in oil, drained

½ cup frozen peas

2 tablespoons freshly grated Parmesan cheese

fresh fennel fronds and slices, to garnish

salt and pepper

1. Heat the oil in a medium saucepan. Add the onion, bacon, and fennel and cook for 5 minutes, until tender.

2. Add the mushrooms and rice and stir well to coat the grains with the oil. Add the tomatoes, tomato paste, stock, lemon zest and juice and season to taste with Tabasco sauce, salt, and pepper.

3. Bring to a boil, stirring, then reduce the heat, cover, and cook gently for 5 minutes.

4. Flake the tuna with a fork and add it to the rice mixture with the peas. Continue cooking for 5–8 minutes, until most of the liquid has been absorbed and the rice grains are tender.

5. Place the risotto in a warmed serving dish, sprinkle with Parmesan, and garnish with fennel fronds and slices.

Roasted Monkfish and Pepper Risotto

Roasted vegetables, especially peppers, have a delicious sweet flavor that goes well with meaty monkfish and rice.

3 red bell peppers, cored, seeded, and cut into large chunks

2 small red onions, cut into thin wedges

½ cup olive oil

4 garlic cloves, crushed

¼ cup chopped oregano

1 pound monkfish

¼ cup butter

1¾ cups risotto rice

⅔ cup dry white wine

5½ cups hot Fish Stock (see page 16)

½ cup dry vermouth, (optional)

salt and pepper

oregano sprig, to garnish

1. Scatter the peppers and onion wedges in a large roasting pan. Mix the oil with the garlic and oregano, season with salt and pepper, and toss with the peppers and onions. Roast in a preheated oven at 425°F for 20 minutes, until they begin to brown.

2. Meanwhile, cut the monkfish fillets away from the central bone and pat dry on paper towels. Slice into small chunks and add to the roasting pan, tossing the ingredients together. Return to the oven for a further 15–20 minutes, until the vegetables are roasted and the fish is cooked through.

3. While the fish is roasting, melt the butter in a large, heavy-based frying pan. Add the rice and stir well to coat the grains with the butter. Add the wine, bring to a boil, and cook, stirring, until almost all the liquid has evaporated. Add the hot stock, a large ladleful at a time, stirring until each addition is absorbed into the rice. Continue adding stock in this way, cooking until the rice is creamy but the grains are still firm. This should take about 20 minutes.

4. Stir the roasted ingredients, any roasting juices and the vermouth, if using, into the risotto. Season to taste with salt and pepper and serve garnished with an oregano sprig.

Red Snapper and Bacon Risotto

Snapper has delicate yet firm flesh with a truly wonderful flavor. If you are buying whole snapper or they are being filleted for you, make sure you keep the heads and bones, as they are rich in gelatine and make excellent stock.

4 large or 8 small red snapper fillets

¼ cup butter

2 tablespoons olive oil

5 ounces smoked bacon, thinly sliced

2 small leeks, chopped

1¾ cups risotto rice

2 garlic cloves, crushed

5½ cups hot Fish Stock (see page 16)

⅓ cup chopped fennel

salt and pepper

red chili slices, to garnish (optional)

1. Pat the fish dry on paper towels and season lightly with salt and pepper. Melt 1 tablespoon of the butter in a frying pan with the oil and fry the fish fillets for 1–2 minutes on each side, until cooked through. Remove from the pan and set aside.

2. Melt the remaining butter in a large, heavy-based saucepan. Add the bacon and cook for 3–4 minutes, until browned. Remove with a slotted spoon. Add the leeks to the pan and cook gently for 2 minutes. Add the rice to the pan and stir well to coat the grains with the butter.

3. Return the bacon to the pan and add the garlic. Add the hot stock, a large ladleful at a time, stirring until each addition is absorbed into the rice. Continue adding stock in this way, cooking until the rice is creamy but the grains are still firm. This should take about 20 minutes.

4. Add the fennel and a little pepper and gently fold in the fish fillets. Heat for 1 minute before serving. Serve garnished with some red chili slices, if desired.

Thai-style Crab Risotto

This risotto tastes best when made with fresh crab meat, but you could use thawed, frozen crab meat if necessary.

⅓ cup coconut cream

1 lemon grass stalk

⅓ cup sunflower oil

1 bunch of scallions, sliced

3 garlic cloves, sliced

1-inch piece of fresh ginger, peeled and chopped

1¾ cups risotto rice

5½ cups hot Fish Stock (see page 16)

¼ cup lime juice

1 small fresh prepared crab

salt and pepper

chopped cilantro leaves, to serve

red chili slices, to garnish

1. Bruise the lemon grass with a rolling pin and slice as thinly as possible.

2. Heat the oil in a large, heavy-based saucepan. Add the scallions, lemon grass, garlic, and ginger and sauté for 3 minutes. Add the rice and stir well to coat the grains with the oil.

3. Add the hot stock, a large ladleful at a time, stirring until each addition is absorbed into the rice. Continue adding stock in this way, cooking until the rice is creamy but the grains are still firm. This should take about 20 minutes. Add the coconut cream with the last of the stock.

4. Add the lime juice and crab, stirring to break it up and heat through. Cover and leave the risotto to rest for a few minutes before serving, scattered with plenty of cilantro and garnished with chili slices.

Squid Risotto

The key to success with squid is to cook it quickly, otherwise it becomes rubbery
and inedible.

1 pound prepared squid tubes

¼ cup butter

2 garlic cloves, crushed

1 onion, chopped

2 cups risotto rice

5½ cups hot Fish Stock (see page 16)

1 tablespoon chopped flat leaf parsley

⅓ cup capers, rinsed

finely grated zest of 2 lemons

salt and pepper

1. Slice the squid into rings and pat dry on paper towels. Melt the butter in a
   large heavy-based saucepan. Add the squid and garlic and sauté gently for
   3–4 minutes, until the squid puffs up. Remove from the pan with a slotted spoon.

2. Add the onion to the pan and sauté gently for 5 minutes, until softened but not
   colored. Add the hot stock, a large ladleful at a time, stirring until each addition is
   absorbed into the rice. Continue adding stock in this way, cooking until the rice is
   creamy but the grains are still firm. This should take about 20 minutes.

3. Return the squid and any cooking juices to the pan with the parsley, capers, and
   lemon zest and season to taste with salt and pepper. Heat through for 1 minute,
   cover, and leave the risotto to rest for a few minutes before serving.

Serves 4/ Preparation time: 10 minutes/ Cooking time: 30 minutes

Anchovy and Tomato Risotto

If you find anchovies too salty, soak them in a little milk, then pat dry before using. In any case, be careful when you add seasoning, as extra salt may not be needed.

¼ cup butter

1 onion, chopped

1 small leek, diced

2 cups risotto rice

⅓ cup sun-dried tomato paste

5½ cups hot Fish Stock (see page 16)

1 2-ounce can anchovies, drained and chopped

1 pound tomatoes, seeded and sliced

small handful flat leaf parsley, chopped

salt and pepper

flat leaf parsley sprigs, to garnish

1. Melt the butter in a large, heavy-based saucepan. Add the onion and leek and sauté for 5 minutes, until softened. Add the rice and stir well to coat the grains with the butter. Stir in the tomato paste.

2. Add the hot stock, a large ladleful at a time, stirring until each addition is absorbed into the rice. Continue adding stock in this way, cooking until the rice is creamy but the grains are still firm. This should take about 20 minutes.

3. Add the anchovies to the pan with the tomato pieces and parsley and season to taste with salt and pepper, if required. Heat through for 1 minute, cover and leave the risotto to rest for a few minutes before serving garnished with parsley sprigs.

Mussel Risotto

2 pounds fresh mussels

¼ cup butter

1 fennel bulb, chopped

⅔ cup dry white wine

2 garlic cloves, crushed

1¾ cups risotto rice

6 large thyme sprigs

1 teaspoon medium-hot curry paste

5 cups hot Fish Stock (see page 16)

⅓ cup heavy cream

salt and pepper

chopped parsley, to garnish

1. Scrub the mussels, discarding any with damaged shells or that do not close when sharply tapped. Melt 1 tablespoon of the butter in a large saucepan. Add the fennel and sauté for 3 minutes. Add the wine and bring to a boil.

2. Place the mussels in the pan and cover tightly. Cook over a high heat, shaking the pan occasionally, for about 5 minutes, until the shells have opened. Drain the mussels, reserving the cooking juices. Shell about half the mussels.

3. Melt the remaining butter in a large heavy-based saucepan. Add the garlic, rice, thyme, and curry paste and cook for 1 minute, stirring. Add the reserved cooking juices and cook, stirring, until the juices have been absorbed by the rice.

4. Add the hot stock, a large ladleful at a time, stirring until each addition is absorbed into the rice. Continue adding stock in this way, cooking until the rice is creamy but the grains are still firm. This should take about 20 minutes. Stir in the cream and all the mussels and cook for 1 minute. Season to taste with salt and pepper, cover and leave the risotto to rest for a few minutes before serving, sprinkled with parsley.

Shrimp, Asparagus, and Olive Risotto

A luxurious risotto with some unusual and subtle flavors, this makes a good dinner party dish. Olive paste is available from Italian delicatessens and many supermarkets, alternatively you can make your own (see page 13).

2½ cups water

1 pound asparagus spears, cut into
  2-inch lengths

¾ cup olive oil

4 shallots, chopped

2 garlic cloves, crushed

2 teaspoons chopped thyme

1¾ cups risotto rice

⅔ cup dry white wine

2½ cups hot Vegetable Stock (see page 19)

1 pound small raw shrimp, peeled

½ cup olive paste (pasta di olive)

⅓ cup torn basil leaves

Parmesan cheese shavings, to serve

1. Bring the water to a boil in a large saucepan. Add the asparagus and cook for 3 minutes. Strain, reserving the liquid, and immediately refresh the asparagus under cold water. Drain well and set aside.

2. Heat the oil in a large frying pan. Add the shallots, garlic, and thyme and sauté for 5 minutes. Add the rice and stir well to coat the grains with the oil. Pour in the wine, bring to a boil, and cook, stirring, until almost all the liquid has evaporated.

3. Meanwhile, put the reserved asparagus liquid and vegetable stock into a small saucepan and bring to a very low simmer. Add the hot stock to the frying pan, a large ladleful at a time, stirring until each addition is absorbed into the rice. Continue adding stock in this way, cooking until the rice is creamy but the grains are still firm. This should take about 20 minutes.

4. Add the shrimp and the asparagus to the rice with the final addition of stock and stir for a further 5 minutes, until the shrimp and rice are cooked. Stir in the olive paste and basil and season to taste with salt and pepper. Cover and leave the risotto to rest for a few minutes before serving with plenty of Parmesan shavings.

Shrimp and Fennel Risotto

The sweet anise flavor of fennel gives this risotto a delicious piquancy.

1 pound raw shrimp in their shells

1 small fennel bulb, sliced

4 parsley sprigs

½ onion, roughly chopped

1 small carrot, roughly chopped

4½ cups water

1¼ cups dry white wine

½ cup butter

¼ cup olive oil

2½ cups risotto rice

1 garlic clove, crushed

grated zest of ½ lemon

fennel fronds, chopped

¼ cup freshly grated Parmesan cheese

salt and pepper

1. Peel the shrimp and reserve the shells and heads. Put the shells, heads, and any roe into a large saucepan. Add the fennel, parsley, onion, carrot, and water. Bring to a boil, then simmer gently for 25–30 minutes.

2. Strain the stock, measure, and make up to 7 cups with the white wine and extra water if necessary. Bring to a boil in a clean pan and simmer gently.

3. Melt half the butter with the oil in a large heavy-based saucepan. Add the rice and stir well to coat the grains with the butter and oil. Add the hot stock, a large ladleful at a time, stirring until each addition is absorbed into the rice. Continue adding stock in this way, cooking until the rice is creamy but the grains are still firm. This should take about 20 minutes. Season to taste with salt and pepper.

4. Melt the remaining butter in a small pan, and stir in the shrimp, garlic, lemon zest, and fennel fronds. Stir into the rice with the Parmesan. Cover and leave the risotto to rest for a few minutes before serving.

Pea and Shrimp Risotto

1 pound raw shrimp

½ cup butter

1 onion, finely chopped

2 garlic cloves, crushed

1¼ cups risotto rice

3 cups shelled peas

⅔ cup dry white wine

6¼ cups hot Vegetable Stock (see page 19)

½ cup chopped mint

salt and pepper

1. Peel the shrimp, reserving the heads and shells.
2. Melt half of the butter in a large frying pan. Add the shrimp heads and shells and stir-fry for 3–4 minutes. Strain the butter and return it to the pan.
3. Add a further 2 tablespoons of the butter to the pan. Add the onion and garlic and sauté for 5 minutes, until softened but not colored. Add the rice and stir well to coat the grains with the butter. Add the peas, then pour in the wine. Bring to a boil, and cook, stirring, until reduced by half.
4. Add the hot stock, a large ladleful at a time, stirring until each addition is absorbed into the rice. Continue adding stock in this way, cooking until the rice is creamy, but the grains are still firm. This should take about 20 minutes.
5. Melt the remaining butter and stir-fry the shrimp for 3–4 minutes, then stir them into the rice with the pan juices and mint and season to taste with salt and pepper. Cover the pan and leave the risotto to rest for a few minutes before serving.

3 Meat and Poultry

Chorizo and Sun-dried Tomato Risotto

¼ cup butter

2 tablespoons olive oil

5 ounces chorizo sausage, thinly sliced

⅔ cup pine nuts

1 red onion, finely chopped

1 small red chili, cored, seeded, and thinly
   sliced

2 bay leaves

2 cups risotto rice

5½ cups hot Chicken Stock (see page 17)

3 ounces sun-dried tomatoes in oil, drained and
   thinly sliced

small handful of cilantro leaves, roughly
   chopped

salt and pepper

mixed leaf salad, to serve (optional)

1. Melt the butter with the oil in a large, heavy-based saucepan. Add the chorizo and pine nuts and fry for 2 minutes, or until the sausage begins to color. Remove the chorizo and nuts with a slotted spoon.

2. Add the onion, chili, and bay leaves to the pan and sauté for 2 minutes. Add the rice and stir well to coat the grains with the butter and oil.

3. Add the hot stock, a large ladleful at a time, stirring until each addition is absorbed into the rice. Continue adding stock in this way, cooking until the rice is creamy but the grains are still firm. This should take about 20 minutes.

4. Return the chorizo and pine nuts to the pan and stir in the sun-dried tomatoes and cilantro leaves. Cook for 1 minute. Cover and leave the risotto to rest for a few minutes before serving with a mixed leaf salad, if liked.

Sage and Lentil Risotto with Herb Sausages

¾ cup Puy lentils

8 herb sausages

¼ cup butter

2 onions, sliced

1¾ cups risotto rice

5 cups hot Chicken Stock (see page 17)

8 large sage leaves, finely shredded, plus extra
    to garnish (optional)

salt and pepper

1. Rinse the lentils, put them in a saucepan, and cover with water. Bring to a boil and simmer for about 25 minutes, until tender. While the lentils are simmering, cook the sausages in a preheated oven at 400°F for 20 minutes, or until golden.

2. Meanwhile, melt the butter in a large heavy-based saucepan. Add the onions and sauté for 5 minutes, until softened but not colored. Add the rice and stir well to coat the grains with the butter.

3. Add the shredded sage leaves to the rice. Add the hot stock, a large ladleful at a time, stirring until each addition is absorbed into the rice. Continue adding stock in this way, cooking until the rice is creamy but the grains are still firm. This should take about 20 minutes.

4. Drain the lentils and add to the pan. Season to taste with salt and pepper, cover and leave the risotto to rest for a few minutes before serving. Top with the sausages and serve garnished with sage leaves, if desired.

Serves 4/ Preparation time: 10 minutes/ Cooking time: 50 minutes

Roasted Pork, Parsnip, and Apple Risotto

This makes a delicious change from a traditional Sunday dinner.

14 ounces boneless, lean pork belly or pancetta

14 ounces slender parsnips

¼ cup sunflower oil

2 Granny Smith apples, peeled, cored, and
    thickly sliced

¼ cup butter

1 onion, chopped

1¾ cups risotto rice

6 large sage leaves, shredded

⅔ cup dry white wine

5 cups hot Chicken Stock (see page 17)

salt and pepper

1. Thinly slice the pork belly or roughly chop the pancetta. Quarter the parsnips lengthwise and toss with the meat and oil in a large roasting pan. Bake in a preheated oven at 425°F for 25 minutes, until beginning to color. Add the apple slices, stir to combine and roast for a further 20–25 minutes until golden.

2. Meanwhile, melt the butter in a large, heavy-based saucepan. Add the onion and sauté gently for 5 minutes, until softened but not colored. Add the rice and sage and stir well to coat the grains with the butter. Add the wine, bring to a boil, and cook, stirring, until almost all the liquid has evaporated.

3. Add the hot stock, a large ladleful at a time, stirring until each addition is absorbed into the rice. Continue adding stock in this way, cooking until the rice is creamy but the grains are still firm. This should take about 20 minutes.

4. Transfer the ingredients from the roasting pan into the risotto, season to taste with salt and pepper and stir together for 1 minute. Cover and leave the risotto to rest for a few minutes before serving.

Pepperoni and Wilted Spinach Risotto

¼ cup butter

2 tablespoons olive oil

3½ ounces pepperoni sausage, thinly sliced

½ cup pine nuts

2 tablespoons paprika

2 garlic cloves, crushed

1¾ cups risotto rice

5 cups hot Chicken Stock (see page 17)

8 ounces baby spinach leaves

⅔ cup raisins

salt and pepper

1. Melt the butter with the oil in a large, heavy-based saucepan. Add the sausage and pine nuts and cook gently for about 3 minutes, or until the pine nuts are golden. Drain with a slotted spoon.
2. Add the paprika, garlic and rice to the pan and stir well to coat the grains with the butter and oil. Add the hot stock, a large ladleful at a time, stirring until each addition is absorbed into the rice. Continue adding stock in this way, cooking until the rice is creamy but the grains are still firm. This should take about 20 minutes.
3. Return the sliced sausage and pine nuts to the pan along with the spinach and raisins. Cook over a gentle heat, stirring the spinach into the rice until wilted. Season to taste with salt and pepper. Cover and leave the risotto to rest for a few minutes before serving.

Serves 4/ Preparation time: 10 minutes/ Cooking time: 35 minutes

Gingered Beef and Walnut Risotto

14 ounces beef fillet

¼ cup butter

1 cup walnut pieces

1 bunch of scallions, chopped

2 garlic cloves, chopped

1¾ cups risotto rice

5½ cups hot Chicken or Vegetable Stock (see pages 17 and 19)

2 tablespoons of fresh ginger, peeled and grated

¼ cup sunflower oil

2 tablespoons soy sauce

7 ounces pak choi, roughly sliced

¼ cup water

salt and pepper

1. Pat the meat dry on paper towels and season with salt and pepper.
2. Melt the butter in a large, heavy-based saucepan. Add the walnuts and cook, stirring until beginning to brown. Remove with a slotted spoon. Add the scallions and cook for 1 minute.
3. Add the garlic and rice to the pan and stir well to coat the grains with the butter. Add the hot stock, a large ladleful at a time, stirring until each addition is absorbed into the rice. Continue adding stock in this way, cooking until the rice is creamy but the grains are still firm. This should take about 20 minutes. Add the grated ginger with the last of the stock.
4. Meanwhile, heat the oil in a frying pan and gently cook the meat, turning frequently, for 10 minutes, until well browned. Remove from the heat and spoon the soy sauce over the meat.
5. Stir the pak choi into the risotto and season to taste with salt and pepper. Cover the risotto and leave to rest for a few minutes. Meanwhile, drain the meat and slice as thinly as possible. Pile the risotto on plates and serve with the meat and walnuts. Stir the water into the frying pan, scraping up any browned bits from the bottom. Spoon over the meat and serve.

Parma Ham and Sweet Potato Risotto

Although Parma ham and other types of prosciutto are expensive, their flavor is unique and irreplaceable.

2 medium sweet potatoes, scrubbed

¼ cup butter

1 bunch of scallions, finely sliced

1¾ cups risotto rice

2 bay leaves

5 cups hot Chicken or Vegetable Stock (see pages 17 and 19)

⅓ cup olive oil

3 ounces Parma ham, cut into pieces

2 tablespoons chopped mixed herbs, such as parsley, chervil, tarragon, and chives

salt and pepper

1. Cut the potatoes into ½-inch chunks and cook in lightly salted, boiling water for 2–3 minutes to soften. Drain and set aside.

2. Melt the butter in a large, heavy-based saucepan. Add the scallions and sauté for 1 minute. Add the rice and stir well to coat the grains with the butter.

3. Add the bay leaves to the rice. Add the hot stock, a large ladleful at a time, stirring until each addition is absorbed into the rice. Continue adding stock in this way, cooking until the rice is creamy but the grains are still firm. This should take about 20 minutes.

4. Meanwhile, heat 2 tablespoons of the oil in a frying pan and cook the ham until golden. Drain and keep warm. Add the remaining oil and fry the sweet potatoes, turning frequently, for 6–8 minutes, until golden.

5. Add the herbs to the risotto and season to taste with salt and pepper, then add the ham and sweet potatoes, folding in gently. Cover and leave the risotto to rest for a few minutes before serving.

Risotto alla Milanese

Virtually every town and city in northern Italy has its own speciality risotto. This
version from Milan is always served with osso buco.

⅓ cup butter

2 tablespoons olive oil

2 onions, finely diced

2¼ cups risotto rice

4½ cups hot Chicken Stock (see page 17)

½ teaspoon saffron threads

½ cup dry vermouth or dry white wine

½ cup Parmesan cheese, freshly grated

salt and pepper

1. Melt ¼ cup of the butter with the olive oil in a large heavy-based saucepan. Add
the onions and sauté for 5 minutes until softened but not colored.

2. Add the rice to the onions and stir well to coat the grains with the butter.

3. Add the hot stock, a large ladleful at a time, stirring until each addition is
absorbed into the rice. Continue adding stock in this way until you have added
about half, then add the saffron and stir well. Continue adding the stock, cooking
until the rice is creamy but the grains are still firm. This should take about
20 minutes in all.

4. Finally add the vermouth or white wine, Parmesan, and the remaining butter in
small pieces. Season to taste with salt and pepper. Stir well, cover and leave the
risotto to rest for a few minutes before serving.

Serves 4–6/ Preparation time: 15 minutes/ Cooking time: about 1 hour

Risotto alla Fiorentina

¼ cup olive oil

5 tablespoons butter, softened

1 onion, sliced

8 ounces ground beef

4 ounces lambs' kidneys, sliced

1 chicken liver, sliced

13 ounces tomatoes, skinned and mashed

2 cups risotto rice

4½ cups hot Beef Stock (see page 18)

⅓ cup Parmesan cheese, freshly grated

salt and pepper

1. Heat the oil and half the butter in a heavy-based saucepan. Add the onion and sauté gently for 5 minutes, until softened but not colored. Add the ground beef, kidneys, and chicken liver, increase the heat and cook, stirring, until browned. Add the tomatoes and season to taste with salt and pepper, lower the heat, and cook for 30 minutes.

2. Add the rice and stir well to coat the grains with the butter and oil. Add the hot stock, a large ladleful at a time, stirring until each addition is absorbed into the rice. Continue adding stock in this way, cooking until the rice is creamy but the grains are still firm. This should take about 20 minutes.

3. Remove the pan from the heat. Stir in the remaining butter and the Parmesan and fold gently to mix. Cover and leave the risotto to rest for a few minutes before serving.

Chestnut, Bacon, and Thyme Risotto

Chestnuts play an important role in the traditional cooking of both Tuscany and Liguria.

⅓ cup olive oil

1 onion, finely chopped

3 garlic cloves, finely chopped

4 slices Canadian bacon or prosciutto, diced

4 ounces cooked, peeled chestnuts,
   roughly chopped

2 cups risotto rice

¼ cup chopped thyme

½ cup dry sherry or white wine

5 cups hot Vegetable Stock (see page 19)

¼ cup freshly grated Parmesan cheese, plus
   extra to garnish

salt and pepper

pat of butter, to garnish (optional)

green salad, to serve (optional)

1. Heat the oil in a frying pan. Add the onion and garlic and sauté for 5 minutes, until softened but not colored. Add the bacon or prosciutto and cook for a further 5–6 minutes, until the bacon is crisp and just starting to brown.

2. Add the chestnuts and the rice to the frying pan and stir well to coat the grains with the oil. Stir in the thyme and sherry.

3. Add the hot stock, a large ladleful at a time, stirring until each addition is absorbed into the rice. Continue adding stock in this way, cooking until the rice is creamy but the grains are still firm. This should take about 20 minutes.

4. Stir the grated Parmesan into the risotto and season to taste with salt and pepper. Cover and leave to rest for a few minutes before serving, garnished with extra Parmesan, plus a pat of butter, if you like. Serve with a green salad, if desired.

Fava Bean, Pancetta, and Fontina Risotto

An everyday Italian cheese, fontina is used here with Parmesan to give a good flavor to this fava bean risotto.

⅓ cup olive oil

1 onion, finely chopped

3 garlic cloves, crushed

3 ounces pancetta, chopped

1¼ cups risotto rice

½ teaspoon dried mixed herbs

3¾ cups hot Chicken or Vegetable Stock (see pages 17 and 19)

1 cup fava beans, thawed if frozen

¾ cup peas

3 ounces fontina cheese, coarsely grated

¼ cup butter

¼ cup freshly grated Parmesan cheese, plus extra shavings to serve

2 tablespoons chopped mint leaves

6–8 basil leaves, torn, plus extra to serve

salt and pepper

1. Heat the olive oil in a large saucepan. Add the onion and sauté for 5 minutes, until softened but not colored. Add the crushed garlic and pancetta to the pan and cook until the pancetta is golden brown. Add the rice and stir well to coat the grains with the oil.

2. With the pan still over a medium heat, add the dried mixed herbs and the hot stock to the rice and bring the mixture to a boil, stirring constantly. Season to taste with salt and pepper. Reduce to a simmer and simmer for 10 minutes, stirring frequently. Add the fava beans and peas to the pan and continue to cook for a further 10 minutes.

3. Remove the pan from the heat and stir in the grated fontina. Dot the butter on top with the grated Parmesan. Cover and leave the risotto to rest for a few minutes.

4. Remove the lid and add the chopped mint and torn basil and gently stir the cheese, butter, and herbs through the risotto. Serve immediately with basil leaves and extra shavings of Parmesan.

Spiced Lamb Risotto with Apricots

Lamb is quite a rich meat, so it is superbly complemented by the subtle sharpness of the dried fruit in this Moroccan-inspired risotto.

14 ounces lean lamb fillet or boneless leg

¼ cup butter

⅓ cup flaked almonds

2 small onions, chopped

1 celery stick, sliced

1 cinnamon stick, halved

good pinch of saffron threads (optional)

1-inch piece of fresh ginger, peeled and grated

2 garlic cloves, crushed

2 cups risotto rice

5½ cups hot Chicken Stock (see page 17)

**¾ cup ready-to-eat dried apricots,
   thinly sliced**

small handful of cilantro, chopped

salt and pepper

1. Cut the lamb into small dice, trimming off and discarding any fat. Pat dry on paper towels and season with salt and pepper.
2. Melt the butter in a large, heavy-based saucepan. Add the lamb and cook, stirring, for 5 minutes until browned. Remove with a slotted spoon. Add the almonds to the pan and cook gently until golden. Remove and set aside.
3. Add the onions and celery to the pan and sauté gently for 5 minutes. Stir in the cinnamon, saffron, ginger, garlic, and rice and stir well to coat the grains with the butter. Add the hot stock, a large ladleful at a time, stirring until each addition is absorbed into the rice. Continue adding stock in this way, cooking until the rice is creamy but the grains are still firm. This should take about 20 minutes.
4. Return the lamb and almonds to the pan and add the apricots and cilantro. Mix, season to taste with salt and pepper and cook for 1 minute. Cover and leave the risotto to rest for a few minutes before serving.

Wafered Lamb and Mint Risotto

14 ounces lean lamb fillet, very thinly sliced

¼ cup butter

¼ cup olive oil

1 large onion, chopped

3 garlic cloves, chopped

1¾ cups risotto rice

⅔ cup white wine

5 cups hot Vegetable Stock (see page 19)

3½ ounces sugar snap peas, sliced lengthwise

small handful of mint sprigs, roughly chopped

¼ cup freshly grated Parmesan cheese

salt and pepper

1. Trim any fat from the lamb and season with salt and pepper. Melt the butter with the oil in a large, heavy-based saucepan. Add the lamb and cook, stirring frequently, for about 5 minutes, until browned. Remove the lamb and set aside.

2. Add the onion to the pan and sauté gently for 5 minutes until softened. Add the garlic and rice and stir well to coat the grains with the butter and oil. Add the wine, bring to a boil, and cook, stirring until almost all the liquid has evaporated.

3. Add the hot stock, a large ladleful at a time, stirring until each addition is absorbed into the rice. Continue adding stock in this way, cooking until the rice is creamy but the grains are still firm. This should take about 20 minutes.

4. Return the lamb to the pan with the sugar snap peas and mint, and season to taste with salt and pepper. Cook for 1 minute, stirring. Stir in the Parmesan, cover, and leave the risotto to rest for a few minutes before serving.

Serves 4/ Preparation time: 10–15 minutes, plus cooling/ Cooking time: 35 minutes

Chicken and Watercress Risotto Cakes

8 ounces skinless, boneless chicken breasts

¼ cup butter

1 onion, chopped

4 garlic cloves, crushed

1 cup risotto rice

2½ cups hot Chicken or Vegetable Stock (see pages 17 and 19)

⅓ cup Parmesan cheese, freshly grated

3 ounces watercress, tough stalks removed

1 egg, lightly beaten

flour, for dusting

⅓ cup polenta or cornmeal

vegetable oil, for shallow-frying

salad, to serve

1. Finely chop the chicken. Melt the butter in a large, heavy-based saucepan. Add the chicken and cook, stirring frequently, for 2–3 minutes, until cooked through. Remove with a slotted spoon and set aside.

2. Add the onion to the pan and sauté gently for 5 minutes. Add the garlic and rice and stir well to coat the grains with the butter. Add the hot stock, a large ladleful at a time, stirring until each addition is absorbed into the rice. Continue adding stock in this way, cooking until the rice is creamy but the grains are still firm. This should take about 20 minutes. Stir in the Parmesan.

3. Roughly chop the watercress and add to the pan, stirring until it has wilted. Add the cooked chicken and season to taste with salt and pepper. Remove the pan from the heat and leave to cool.

4. Put the beaten egg on a plate. Put the polenta on another plate. Using lightly floured hands, shape the risotto mixture into 8 even-sized pieces. Flatten into cakes and coat first in the beaten egg, then in the polenta.

5. Heat a little vegetable oil in a large frying pan and fry the cakes for about 3 minutes on each side until golden. Drain on paper towels and serve with salad.

Spicy Chicken and Broccoli Risotto

3 tablespoons butter

¼ cup olive oil

2 skinless, boneless chicken breasts, diced

½ onion, very finely chopped

1 garlic clove, finely chopped

1–2 fresh red chilies, seeded, and very finely chopped

1½ cups risotto rice

4½ cups hot Chicken Stock (see page 17)

8 ounces broccoli florets

⅓ cup freshly grated Parmesan cheese

salt and pepper

1. Melt 1 tablespoon of the butter with the oil in a heavy-based saucepan. Add the diced chicken and sauté gently for 2–3 minutes. Add the onion and sauté for 5 minutes, until softened but not colored. Add the garlic and chili and cook until the garlic is golden.

2. Add the rice to the pan and stir well to coat the grains with the butter and oil. Add the hot stock, a large ladleful at a time, stirring until each addition is absorbed into the rice. Continue adding stock in this way, cooking until the rice is creamy but the grains are still firm. This should take about 20 minutes.

3. Plunge the broccoli florets into a pan of boiling water for 1 minute. Drain thoroughly and add to the rice with the Parmesan. Season to taste with salt and pepper and stir in the remaining butter. Cover and leave the risotto to rest for a few minutes before serving.

Serves 4/ Preparation time: 15–20 minutes/ Cooking time: 30 minutes

Chicken Liver Risotto

This recipe cheats a little, but it is much more convenient and less time-consuming than an authentic risotto cooked in the traditional way—and it works very well.

¼ cup extra virgin olive oil

1 onion, finely chopped

8 ounces chicken livers, cores removed, roughly chopped

1 garlic clove, crushed

1½ cups risotto rice

½ cup dry white wine

about 4½ cups hot Chicken Stock (see page 17)

large pinch of saffron threads

1 cup frozen peas or petits pois

¾ cup heavy cream

¼ cup chopped flat leaf parsley (optional)

about ¼ cup thinly shaved Parmesan cheese

salt and pepper

1. Heat the olive oil in a large Dutch oven. Add the onion and sauté over a low heat, stirring frequently, for about 5 minutes, until softened but not colored.
2. Add the chicken livers and the crushed garlic, increase the heat to moderate and cook, stirring constantly, for 2–3 minutes, or until the livers change color on all sides.
3. Add the rice and stir well to coat the grains with the oil. Add the wine and stir until the bubbles subside.
4. Pour in 2½ cups of the hot stock, add the saffron, season to taste with salt and pepper and stir well. Bring to a boil, then cover and simmer over a gentle heat for 10 minutes, stirring occasionally to prevent the rice from sticking to the bottom of the pan.
5. Add a further 1¾ cups hot stock to the risotto, stir well to combine, then add the peas. Cover and simmer for a further 10 minutes, stirring occasionally and adding a little more stock if necessary.
6. Remove the pan from the heat and gently fold in the cream and the parsley, if using. Adjust the seasoning to taste. Serve hot, topped with Parmesan shavings.

Serves 6/ Preparation time: 35 minutes/ Cooking time: 2 hours

Chicken Risotto with White Wine and Tomatoes

Every part of a whole chicken is used in this hearty risotto—as you make the stock before you start to cook the rest of the dish.

2 pounds oven-ready chicken

9 cups water

2 celery sticks

2 onions

2 carrots

⅓–½ cup olive oil

¾ cup white wine

12 ounces tomatoes, skinned and mashed

2½ cups risotto rice

⅓ cup butter, softened

⅓ cup Parmesan cheese, freshly grated

salt and pepper

2–4 tablespoons chopped parsley, to garnish

1. Remove the bones from the chicken and place them in a large pan with the water. Add 1 celery stick, 1 onion, and 1 carrot and season with salt and pepper. Bring to the boil, lower the heat, cover, and simmer for 1½ hours. Strain the stock and keep hot.

2. Meanwhile, dice the chicken meat, removing and discarding all the skin. Finely chop the remaining celery, onion, and carrot. Heat the olive oil, add the chopped vegetables and sauté until lightly colored. Add the chicken and cook, stirring constantly, for a further 5 minutes. Add the wine, bring to a boil, and cook, stirring, until it has evaporated.

3. Add the tomatoes and season to taste with salt and pepper. Cover and cook over a low heat for 20 minutes, adding a little of the hot chicken stock if the mixture becomes dry.

4. Add the rice. Add the hot stock, a large ladleful at a time, stirring until each addition is absorbed into the rice. Continue adding stock in this way, cooking until the rice is creamy but the grains are still firm. This should take about 20 minutes.

5. Remove from the heat, add the butter and Parmesan, and fold in gently. Cover and leave the risotto to rest for a few minutes before serving, sprinkled with parsley.

4 Desserts

Venetian Rice Pudding

¾ cup golden raisins

⅓ cup medium sherry (optional)

2½ cups hot low-fat milk

⅔ cup heavy cream

1 vanilla pod, split lengthwise, or 2 teaspoons
   vanilla extract

¼ cup superfine sugar

½ teaspoon apple pie spice

finely grated zest of 1 lemon

⅔ cup risotto rice

lemon zest strips, to decorate

**This will be a revelation for anyone whose only experience of rice pudding
was cafeteria lunches.**

1. Put the raisins in a bowl with the sherry, if using, and leave to soak while you
   make the risotto. Put the milk in a saucepan with the cream, vanilla pod or
   extract, sugar, spice, and lemon zest and bring almost to a boil.
2. Add the rice and cook on the lowest heat, stirring frequently, for 20–30 minutes or
   until the rice is creamy but the grains are still firm.
3. Stir in the raisins and any sherry from the bowl and serve warm or cold decorated
   with lemon zest strips.

Iced Fig Risotto

This is the perfect dessert to serve at the end of a leisurely supper on a warm summer evening.

2½ cups low-fat milk

3 tablespoons superfine sugar

finely grated zest of 1 orange

⅔ cup risotto rice

butter, for greasing

8 fresh figs

¼ cup clear honey

¼ cup orange juice

½ pint vanilla ice cream

1. Put the milk, sugar, and orange zest in a large saucepan and bring almost to a boil. Add the rice and cook on the lowest possible heat, stirring frequently, for 25–35 minutes or until the rice is creamy but the grains are still firm. Remove from the heat and set aside to cool.

2. Halve the figs and place in a lightly buttered shallow ovenproof dish. Drizzle with the honey and orange juice and bake in a preheated oven at 400°F for about 20 minutes, or until beginning to color.

3. Scoop the ice cream into the rice mixture and stir until it has just melted to make a creamy sauce. Spoon into bowls with the figs and cooking juices and serve immediately.

Strawberry Risotto

8 ounces small strawberries

¼ cup orange-flavored liqueur (optional)

¼ cup superfine sugar, plus 3 tablespoons

2 cups low-fat milk

2 tablespoons unsalted butter

½ cup risotto rice

mint sprigs, to decorate

1. Thinly slice the strawberries and put them in a bowl with the orange-flavored liqueur, if using, and 3 tablespoons sugar. Bring the milk almost to a boil in a saucepan with the remaining sugar.

2. Melt the butter in a large heavy-based saucepan. Add the rice and stir well to coat the grains with the butter. Pour the hot milk over the rice and cook gently on the lowest possible heat, stirring frequently, for about 25–35 minutes or until the rice is creamy but the grains are still firm.

3. Lightly fold the strawberries and juices into the risotto and serve immediately, decorated with mint sprigs.

Blueberry and Vanilla Risotto

Rich and creamy, this fruity dessert is irresistible.

2½ cups hot low-fat milk

¼ cup superfine sugar, plus 2 tablespoons

2 teaspoons vanilla extract

3 tablespoons unsalted butter

⅔ cup risotto rice

1½ cups fresh blueberries

½ cup heavy cream

shortbread or dessert cookies, to serve
  (optional)

1. Put the milk in a saucepan with ¼ cup of the sugar and the vanilla and bring almost to a boil.
2. Meanwhile, melt the butter in a large, heavy-based saucepan. Add the rice and stir well to coat the grains with the butter. Add the hot milk and bring to a boil. Reduce the heat and simmer, stirring frequently, for 25–35 minutes or until the rice is creamy, but the grains are still firm.
3. Gently stir the blueberries into the risotto and spoon into bowls. Spoon over the cream and sprinkle with the remaining sugar. Serve with shortbread or dessert cookies, if desired.

Mascarpone Risotto with Roasted Peaches

Peaches and creamy mascarpone cheese are a classic combination, but you could use nectarines, if you prefer.

2½ cups low-fat milk

¼ cup superfine sugar

3 tablespoons unsalted butter, melted

2 tablespoons confectioner's sugar

3 ripe peaches, thickly sliced

⅔ cup risotto rice

½ cup mascarpone cheese

¼ cup medium sherry

½ cup amaretti or ratafia biscuits, lightly crushed (optional)

1. Put the milk in a saucepan with the sugar and bring almost to a boil.
2. Meanwhile, brush the peaches with the melted butter, sprinkle with confectioner's sugar and cook under a preheated broiler until they are beginning to turn golden brown.
3. Add the rice to the hot milk, bring to a boil and then simmer gently, stirring frequently, for 25–35 minutes or until the rice is creamy but the grains are still firm. Stir in the mascarpone until melted, then stir in the sherry.
4. Spoon the risotto into bowls and top with the peaches. Serve sprinkled with the crushed biscuits, if desired.

Baked Cherry Risotto

2 cups low-fat milk

½ cup superfine sugar

1 teaspoon vanilla extract

½ cup risotto rice

⅔ cup heavy cream

13 ounces fresh cherries, pitted and halved

1. Put the milk in a large, heavy-based saucepan with ¼ cup of the sugar and the vanilla extract. Bring just to a boil. Add the rice, reduce the heat, and simmer very gently, stirring frequently, for 25–35 minutes or until the rice is creamy but the grains are still firm. Remove from the heat and stir in the cream.

2. Scatter the cherries in a 4½-cup shallow ovenproof dish or individual ovenproof dishes. Spoon the risotto over the cherries, spreading it to the edges of the dish.

3. Sprinkle with the remaining sugar and cook under a preheated broiler for 4–5 minutes until the sugar has caramelized. Leave to cool slightly before serving.

Serves 4/ Preparation time: 5–10 minutes/ Cooking time: 25–35 minutes

Dessert Wine Risotto with Florentine Brittle

¼ cup superfine sugar

2 cups water

1 cinnamon stick, halved

1¼ cups sweet dessert wine

⅔ cup risotto rice

⅓ cup heavy cream

FLORENTINE BRITTLE:

vegetable oil, for brushing

2 tablespoons unsalted butter

2 tablespoons superfine sugar

¼ cup flaked almonds

¼ cup raisins

3 glacé cherries, chopped

1 teaspoon all-purpose flour

1. First make the brittle. Lightly oil a baking sheet. Melt the butter in a small saucepan, then stir in the sugar until dissolved. Add the remaining brittle ingredients and stir well. Spoon onto the prepared baking sheet and spread very thinly.

2. Bake in a preheated oven at 350°F for 15–20 minutes until deep golden. Remove from the oven and leave on the baking sheet until cool. Lift from the sheet and transfer to a plate.

3. Meanwhile, make the risotto. Put the sugar in a large, heavy-based saucepan with the water and heat until the sugar dissolves. Add the cinnamon stick, wine, and rice. Bring to a boil, reduce the heat, and simmer gently, stirring frequently, for 25–35 minutes or until the rice is creamy but the grains are still firm.

4. Stir the cream into the risotto and spoon into dishes. Break the Florentine brittle into pieces and scatter over the risotto before serving.

Spiced Risotto Cakes with Plum Compote

Contrasting colors and textures make a simple dessert into a work of art.

2 cups milk

¼ cup superfine sugar

½ teaspoon ground cinnamon

freshly grated nutmeg

⅔ cup risotto rice

1 egg, lightly beaten

¾ cup amaretti biscuits, crushed

all-purpose flour, for dusting

vegetable oil, for frying

mint sprigs, to decorate

lightly whipped cream or crème fraîche,
    to serve (optional)

COMPOTE:

¼ cup superfine sugar

1¼ cups water

finely grated zest and juice of 1 lemon

1 pound plums, halved

1. To make the risotto cakes, put the milk in a large, heavy-based saucepan with the sugar, cinnamon, and nutmeg, and bring almost to a boil. Add the rice, reduce the heat to its lowest setting and simmer gently, stirring frequently, for about 25–35 minutes or until the rice is creamy but the grains are still firm. Remove from the heat and set aside to cool.
2. Meanwhile, to make the compote, put the sugar in a saucepan with the water and heat gently until the sugar dissolves. Add the lemon zest and juice and the plums and simmer gently for about 10 minutes, until the plums are tender.
3. Put the beaten egg on a plate and the crushed biscuits on another. When the risotto is cool enough to handle, shape it into 8 small cakes using lightly floured hands. Coat first in the beaten egg and then in the biscuit crumbs.
4. Heat a ¼ inch of oil in a frying pan and fry the risotto cakes very gently for 1–2 minutes on each side, until golden. Drain on paper towels and serve with the compote, decorated with mint sprigs and accompanied by lightly whipped cream or crème fraîche, if desired.

Serves 4/ Preparation time: 5–10 minutes/ Cooking time: 25–35 minutes

Chocolate Risotto

When you are adding the chocolate to this dessert, try not to overmix it, as the marbled effect looks good.

2½ cups milk

2 tablespoons sugar

¼ cup butter

⅔ cup risotto rice

½ cup hazelnuts, toasted and chopped

½ cup golden raisins

4 ounces good quality dark chocolate, grated

splash of brandy (optional)

grated chocolate, to decorate

1. Put the milk and sugar into a saucepan and heat until almost boiling.
2. Melt the butter in a heavy-based saucepan, add the rice and stir well to coat the grains with the butter.
3. Add the hot milk, a large ladleful at a time, stirring until each addition is absorbed into the rice. Continue adding milk in this way, cooking until the rice is creamy but the grains are still firm. This should take about 25–35 minutes.
4. Finally, add the hazelnuts, raisins, grated chocolate, and a splash of brandy, if using, and mix quickly. Serve decorated with grated chocolate.

Index

Acknowledgments

Senior Editor: Sarah Ford
Senior Designer: Joanna Bennett
Production Controller: Viv Cracknell

Special Photography: William Reavell
Food Stylist: Oona van den Berg

All other photography Octopus Publishing
Group Limited/ David Loftus 23, 39, 42, 109 top
right/ Hilary Moore 104/ Ian Wallace front cover
center, front cover bottom right, 21 bottom center,
26, 29, 30, 31, 33, 37, 41, 45, 48, 59, 78–79, 96/
Philip Webb 56, 57/ Sandra Lane 92/